STRESS-TESTING

YOUR SAVINGS

STRESS-TESTING

YOUR **SAVINGS**

YOUR FINANCIAL GUIDE TO
NAVIGATE TO AND THROUGH
RETIREMENT

KEITH R. GEBERT

Advantage®

Published by Advantage, Charleston, South Carolina.
Member of Advantage Media Group.

ADVANTAGE is a registered trademark, and the Advantage colophon is a trademark of Advantage Media Group, Inc.

Printed in the United States of America.

ISBN: 978-1-59932-719-8
LCCN: 2016957437

Cover design by George Stevens.

This publication is designed to provide accurate and authoritative information in regard to the subject matter covered. It is sold with the understanding that the publisher is not engaged in rendering legal, accounting, or other professional services. If legal advice or other expert assistance is required, the services of a competent professional person should be sought.

Advantage Media Group is proud to be a part of the Tree Neutral® program. Tree Neutral offsets the number of trees consumed in the production and printing of this book by taking proactive steps such as planting trees in direct proportion to the number of trees used to print books. To learn more about Tree Neutral, please visit **www.treeneutral.com.**

Advantage Media Group is a publisher of business, self-improvement, and professional development books. We help entrepreneurs, business leaders, and professionals share their Stories, Passion, and Knowledge to help others Learn & Grow. Do you have a manuscript or book idea that you would like us to consider for publishing? Please visit **advantagefamily.com** or call **1.866.775.1696.**

This book is dedicated to the most courageous woman I know, my mother, Sandy. She has demonstrated not only courage but dedication to my family throughout the hardest times of our lives. To me, she is my rock. She is by far the strongest woman I have ever known. She has had many trials in her life and tragedies, yet she overcame all of them and became even stronger than before. As I think back on hard times, I remember the strength she had. She is my inspiration and the reason for me being able to write this book. Mom, nothing can compare to you. You're a gift from above, and I hope this makes you proud. I love you.

This book is also dedicated to my father, Randy, who gives true meaning to the word "survivor." In his relentless fight, despite the odds to survive, he never gave up. Thats how he always lived his life and continues to do so. Your strength and tenacity is like no other and I'm proud to know that I have my father's genes. Thats how I got this far. So, thank you Dad. You're my superhero.

To my two sisters, Tammy and Nicole. I couldn't have asked for anything more than you two older sisters. The love, support, guidance, and protection you gave me as your littler brother reassured me that I can take on any challenge and you would be right there with me. Thank you to the two greatest big sisters anyone can have.

To my nieces and nephews, Brianna, Alexis, Joey, and Jayden. I hope this book sets an example for you in many ways. For one, if you put your mind to it, you can accomplish anything you want in life. You were born into a family of strength and wisdom. I will always be here to guide you and protect you on your journey.

For my grandfather and uncle who could not be here today to read this book. I know for all the times I wanted to quit, you gave me the wind beneath me to push on.

In loving memory of my Grandfather Sonny and Uncle Benny. I hope I made you proud.

All proceeds from this book will go to the Make-A-Wish Foundation of New Jersey.

ACKNOWLEDGMENT

Thank you to John P. DeSantis, LLM (Taxation), CPA, for his contribution to this book in chapter 5, Estate Planning Essentials. John is the managing member of the law firm of Levine DeSantis, LLC, in Springfield, New Jersey. He concentrates his practice in estate, gift, and generation-skipping planning for individuals and families, as well as in multigenerational planning for closely held businesses.

TABLE OF CONTENTS

ABOUT THE AUTHOR

Keith Gebert is the CEO of RightBridge Financial Group. He has ten years of experience in the investment and insurance industry. Keith holds his Series 7, 63, and 65 licenses, as well as life, health, and annuity licenses in New York, New Jersey, Florida, Connecticut, and North Carolina. Keith has been featured in *The Wall Street Journal* and on CNBC, MSNBC, and Fox Business News. He was born and raised in New York City but now resides in New Jersey. An active philanthropist, Keith is a "Wishmaker" with the Make-A-Wish Foundation of New Jersey, and works with the USO, St. Jude's Children's Hospital, and the Humane Society of the United States.

INTRODUCTION

We all want our lives to be as fulfilling and secure as possible; we want to know that our bodies, our relationships, and our finances are in the best shape possible. These three aspects of our lives—physical, social/emotional, and financial—are interrelated. Each affects the others; and all of them have a huge impact on our future.

In newspapers and on the news, you'll notice that more and more medical experts today are realizing that good health requires a holistic, whole-body perspective. You can't focus on only one body part if you expect to achieve overall physical health; you need to understand how cardiac health impacts circulatory health, how digestive health affects neurological health, and how your emotions interact with your overall health—and vice versa. This same interactive, 360-degree approach applies to your financial health. If something is missing or malfunctioning in the system, even something that seems small and inconsequential, your entire financial future could be thrown out of balance.

In fact, physical health and financial health are more closely related than you might think. Both greatly impact your current and future happiness, well-being, and activity levels. Both require you to see the big picture in order to see where the potential problems are.

You can't just do one thing—like taking a daily vitamin or saving in a 401(k), for example—and expect that to be enough to ensure your overall physical or financial health. By the same token, it doesn't work to "cure" a physical or financial "symptom" if there's a larger, more serious underlying problem that's growing worse and worse.

As the CEO of RightBridge Financial Group, I have spent the last decade helping individuals, couples, and families make sounder investment and insurance decisions by essentially "stress-testing" their financial plans. In the chapters that follow, we will examine your entire financial picture, step by step. Much like a medical practitioner, I'll help you to see where your strengths and weakness lie and suggest courses of treatment that would better ensure your future well-being. With a stronger understanding of your options, you will be able to strengthen your financial plan, avoid costly mistakes, and better anticipate financial stressors to keep them from throwing you off your financial course.

CHAPTER 1

WHY YOU NEED A TRUSTED ADVISOR

One summer, I took a trip with some family and friends to Whistler, British Columbia. We decided to go rafting on the glacier-fed Elaho River, which many consider to be one of the most dangerous whitewater rafting rivers in the world. So naturally, I was very nervous when we got on the raft, although the water seemed calm. However, within about ten minutes, we found ourselves in a level five rapid.

While we plummeted down the river, it occurred to me who the most important person on that raft was—the guide. Why? Because he possessed both the knowledge and experience to navigate the rough waters. He knew the path to take to help get us safely down the river. Similarly, the right financial professional or "guide" can lead you down the right path through retirement.

I can't tell you how often I hear people say, "My uncle [or cousin or neighbor] says you don't need a financial advisor. He manages his money himself, and he retired when he was forty-five—and he's rich!"

It's hard to stop myself. I often step into the conversation and say, "Well, are *you* rich?" and when they shake their heads, I continue, "And do you have thirty to forty hours a week to sit and watch the stock market, analyze strategies, learn what oil prices do to the economy, learn what the currency is doing, learn what imports and exports are doing and how they're shaping the overall economy, and learn what effect war has on the market?"

Every one of them admits that they don't have the time.

"Well, then I guess you better ask your rich uncle to help you out," I say. "Otherwise you need a financial advisor."

If they *still* don't look convinced, I say, "You know, your rich uncle who retired at forty-five? He can probably afford to lose a little money in retirement. But if you can't, you better hire a professional— someone who does this for a living—to give you some advice."

Whether you are a doctor, an attorney, or an engineer—no matter what your area of expertise—you might assume that you can do more of the same with your finances. You're used to thinking of yourself as an expert—and you *are*. But that doesn't mean you can possibly know as much as someone who trained to be a financial advisor and has years of experience. That's no criticism of your expertise in your own field; it's just an acknowledgment that in today's complicated world we need specialists. None of us has time to learn *everything*; nor do we have time to *do* everything.

If you need surgery, you will definitely want a surgeon; if you're building a house, you'll need an architect and a carpenter—someone who has trained to do the job you'd never dream of doing yourself. And ideally, you want to pick from surgeons or architects who have years of experience and a proven track record in their field. Well, the same principle applies to your finances.

When it comes to your physical health, there may be lots of situations where you feel you have enough knowledge and experience to handle minor illnesses. If you have a cold or you cut your finger, you pretty much know what action to take. After all, you're an intelligent adult, and you've been doing a good job keeping yourself healthy for many years. By the same token, I have a lot of folks say to me, "We've always managed our own portfolio—and we're happy with the results," and often when I take a look, I wholeheartedly agree: they have a good portfolio, and they've done a good job managing it.

As we get older, all of us sooner or later run into some form of health crisis. Our bodies have far different needs at sixty and seventy than when we were thirty and forty. Whether it's a heart attack, arthritis, or a serious illness like cancer, inevitably each of us encounters a medical situation we can't handle on our own. We can't take a couple of Tylenol, drink plenty of fluids, and get some extra rest. It doesn't matter how great an expert we are in our own professional field, we still need doctors—trained experts in their professional field.

The same applies to your finances. You may have managed just fine when you were younger, but as time goes by, the odds increase that you'll run into something unexpected, the way my own parents did. Some sort of crisis is inevitable, and you have to be prepared. Even if you weather a crisis, you will find as you get nearer to retirement that your financial needs will change. Without the help of a professional, you could find yourself at the brink of retirement with a major financial crisis on your hands—just as my family did—without a way forward.

When it comes to unexpected financial burdens, my family and I can definitely speak from experience. On a fall day in 1992, when I was eight years old, my family's life changed forever because of a serious accident that hospitalized my father. As a result, my family faced not only an emotional crisis but also a serious financial one. We depended on my father's income, and with him in the hospital my mother had to quickly find a way to manage without his weekly paychecks. My father's body was broken—and so were our finances. She could have used some good financial counseling.

Unfortunately, that sort of advice wasn't available to her at the time. No one told her how to find an income source to pay for the medical bills; no one showed her how to invest their savings safely. And remember, the early 1990s were not a great time for most people to invest in the stock market.

The sad thing was that my mom was no stranger to the financial industry. She was a bond transfer agent at E.F. Hutton and Dean Witter, the stock brokerage firm, so she knew about investments. She was also well aware of the stock market's fluctuations. But without a good financial advisor in her corner to help guide her through some difficult financial choices, she was too overwhelmed by the personal crisis that hit our family to think clearly about our family's finances.

Although we made it through that challenging period with my father in the hospital, we learned the hard way how difficult it is to make a financial plan by ourselves that can withstand life's ups and downs. No matter how savvy you may be about the economy and finances, if you're not a trained professional in this field, you'll need advice—and even if you are a trained financial advisor, you would benefit from an outside perspective.

WHY DO-IT-YOURSELF FINANCIAL MANAGEMENT DOESN'T WORK

I recently met a women through a current client who had been contributing for decades to a 401(k) through her employer. Her account kept increasing in size, and she was happy to leave it all in her employer's hands. She never gave it a thought until the day the company informed its employees that it would no longer be contributing to the account (matching their employees' contribution up to 3 percent of their pay).

"Now, I do a spreadsheet every month and recently realized something," she said. "I don't have as much growth in my portfolio as I thought I did."

The money in her account had grown largely because of the company contributions. Without that, she could see that she wasn't getting much real investment growth.

This woman was an engineer—definitely an expert in her field—but she had made an important realization: "I should have had a financial advisor all these years," she said. "I needed someone who could have recognized the true state of affairs and guided me."

Her story, unfortunately, is all too common. So many intelligent, successful people try to handle their financial situation on their own—but no matter how financially savvy they are, they don't have time to be attentive day by day, minute by minute, to what the stock market is doing. They are doctors, lawyers, and teachers with busy careers; they are stay-at-home moms and single dads. They are very good at their jobs—and because they're good at their jobs, they just don't have time to manage their finances the way they need to be managed.

When it comes right down to it, your full-time job has to be your full-time job! Do what you do well to the best of your ability—and seek professional help with other areas of your life.

A NEW ECONOMY

Professionals who started their careers in the 1960s and 1970s have grown accustomed to a market that was largely on a bull run all the way through 2014. There were some major dips during those years, but overall, the market performed in a fairly bullish way. So folks who handled their own portfolios during that period have gained a false sense of security when it comes to their investments. They saw overall growth, so they must have been doing something right. Unfortunately, they don't realize that their portfolios may have done well simply because the overall market was on its way steadily up.

Today's market is an entirely different animal. We're in a new economy, one where volatility is the most prominent feature. These days it takes an expert, someone who has been trained to understand and follow all the factors that influence the economy, to make wise investments.

The situation is a lot like a recent flight I was on. Halfway through the flight, the pilot got on the speaker and said, "Ladies and gentlemen, we've put on the seat belt sign. We ask that everyone stay in their seats. We're seeing some turbulence up ahead. There's a storm, but don't worry. Everything's going to be okay."

The ride got pretty bumpy, but as I tightened my grip on the armrests, I had no inclination *whatsoever* to rush up to the cockpit and try to take over. I was just happy to know that an experienced expert was guiding the flight.

Good financial advisors can do the same for you when it comes to your investments. They'll be able to help you get though the bumpiest of financial rides—without making you feel nauseous. They'll be able to say, "Don't worry, everything's going to be okay. Just sit back and think about your destination."

It's not enough to just *say* that, of course. Good financial advisors will be able to *show* you how they are going to guide you safely to your financial future.

"See, here it is on paper, a projection for the next fifteen years," they'll say. "If we see two more recessions like we did in 2008, or another decade of war, this is how things will play out." A strong financial advisor can say that because they have the expertise to analyze previous numbers in order to project how the government spends during wars and how the overall economy is affected during a recession. "This is where your portfolio will be in a worst-case scenario," they'll say. "Maybe we need to change something here or there, but you'll be okay because we have a philosophy in place."

As a do-it-yourselfer, you don't have the same experience and knowledge base a financial advisor does. That means you won't have the ability to take action fast enough to preserve yourself during a down market. As a result, your lifestyle during your retirement years could turn out to be not what you'd hoped.

HOW TO FORTIFY YOUR FINANCIAL HEALTH

I'm not saying that you should just put your finances in an advisor's hands and forget about them. That makes as much sense as thinking that because you see a doctor regularly, you don't have to take any steps to ensure that you have a healthy lifestyle. For optimum well-being in both circumstances, you need to be fully engaged for an optimum outcome.

One way of doing that is to communicate regularly with your financial advisor. I hear people say things like, "I told my broker everything when I met with him, and he knows who I am and what my needs are." When I talk with them a little more, I find out that the last time they talked to their advisor was two years ago—or five or even ten years ago. A lot can change during that time! Children grow up and move out, elderly parents grow older and move in, or an emergency may come up and wipe out your savings. If advisors don't have all the facts about your current circumstances, they won't be able to give you the guidance you need.

Have you ever gone to your yearly physical with your doctor and then as you were driving home said to yourself, "I forgot to mention that I've been having this ache or pain. I wonder if it's anything I should be worried about." Your doctor's not a mind reader; she can't know things you don't tell her. And your financial advisor won't be able to adjust his advice for new circumstances in your life if you don't tell him about them.

Ideally, you need an advisor you feel comfortable communicating with regularly—not just once a year or once every five years. One of the best ways to stay consistently engaged with your financial health is to find an advisor with whom you can build a relationship.

You want someone who will take the time to talk with you, answer your questions, and help you understand what actions he's taking on your behalf. When you're working regularly with someone you trust, you're a lot less likely to run into a surprise.

As you look forward, it only makes sense to do what you can to build your future financial health *now* with the help of a trusted financial advisor, to help ensure that you have many opportunities for happiness and meaningful activity in the years ahead.

After you find a trusted financial advisor, your next step is to work with him or her to build a financial plan.

CHAPTER 2

WHY YOU NEED A
WRITTEN PLAN

My father's accident changed my family's life so drastically because my parents' only financial plan at the time was to set aside savings when they could. Like many people their age, they didn't have a plan in place for the day when they were no longer wage earners. After all, when the accident happened they were still solidly in the phase of their lives we call "growth and accumulation," when retirement still seemed far, far away. So when my father could suddenly no longer go to work, they had no financial safety net to catch them.

They hadn't planned on that accident, of course. And they never thought about how their personal crisis might coincide with a larger political crisis. At the time, back in the early 1990s, the stock market crashed and intensified the impact of dipping into the family savings.

The same terrible accidents and economic swings happen today and will continue far into the future.

The real story is not about how unlucky my family was at the time—in fact, learning the hard way back then has made me who I am today and has helped a lot of my clients' families to weather some difficult times. The lesson here is that a solid financial plan that was stress-tested to withstand tough times would have made a huge difference in our lives.

No matter the economic climate, you need a well-managed financial plan. You never know when the stock market will drop or an emergency will blindside you. Having a plan in place now could mean the difference between financial comfort in the years to come or having your income seriously diminished by an unexpected health crisis or a recession when you're ready to retire.

YOUR FINANCIAL HEALTH PLAN

If you ever developed a health condition that needed long-term care, your medical practitioner would draw up a treatment plan. You would want this plan to be as specific and thought-out as possible, addressing every possible factor that could affect your recovery. You would also want it to be as individualized as possible, addressing your particular needs, rather than being some generalized treatment formula your doctor uses every time he sees someone with a similar condition. Your health-care plan would coordinate all the factors that contribute to your physical health, including things like nutrition and diet, medications, lifestyle, and treatment therapies. It would coordinate the efforts of everyone involved, from nurses to specialists, and it would also spell out clearly what *you* need to do to be healthy. Your health-care plan would make sure that your treatment continued smoothly, without interruption; it would keep you and everyone else on track, so that a month from now or a year from now you would still have a plan to guide you toward well-being. At the same time, this plan could be reviewed periodically and adjusted as your health needs changed. If you had a miraculous recovery, you might be able to discontinue some medications, while if you had a setback, your doctor might want to increase those medications or try something different.

A financial plan serves a very similar purpose. It takes into account the financial factors that are unique to your situation and builds an individualized plan around them to address problems and help you achieve financial well-being. Your financial plan is a useful document not only for you and your advisor but also for other professionals involved, such as your accountant and lawyer. Like a health-care plan, your financial plan takes a long-term perspective, but it also needs to be reviewed frequently and adjusted as needed as circumstances change.

WHAT *ISN'T* A FINANCIAL PLAN

When I meet with new clients, I always ask, "What does your financial plan look like? Did you bring the written plan with you today?"

They usually say one of two things: either "No, I don't have a financial plan" or "Is this it?"—and then they hand me either their monthly financial statements or an analysis from their broker of their portfolio's performance over the past ten or twenty years. They have no idea what a financial plan should look like, and no one has ever educated them. If they do have something like a financial plan, it's usually at least five to ten years old, which means it's no longer a viable road map for their retirement plans.

If you've been going to any of the big Wall Street firms, you should understand that you usually won't get a financial plan that was custom-made for you. Instead, you'll probably get some cookie-cutter-designed booklet that has your names added into it; along with it, you'll likely get something that's called "your risk tolerance," which will be based on a questionnaire you've answered. Everything else will be a bunch of computerized analytics that look pretty much exactly the same for every one of the firm's clients. If your doctor took the same approach to your health-care plan, you'd probably feel uneasy about the quality of care you'd be getting—and you should!

When a client comes in with a "financial plan" that resembles a generic handout, I always get curious about the real state of their affairs. I often ask questions like, "Do you know where you'll be drawing income from during retirement?" "Do you know the most tax-efficient way to take that?" "Do you know if you're taking too much or unnecessary income that's affecting your tax bracket—or your ability to get medical insurance, based on reported income?" There are a host of different areas where I can go in and help clients tweak things to their advantage.

Usually clients don't know the answers to these questions. They say something along the lines of: "My broker handles all that. I let him worry about the details."

My clients walk into my office knowing they need help; they just don't know what kind of help they need. By the time they walk out the door, I want to be sure they have a far better understanding of their finances. I'll send them home with some homework so that the next time we meet we can sit down and work out their real financial plan. They'll need to bring me the answers to a whole set of questions, such as:

- What is the end result I am hoping for from my financial plan?

- What will my expenses be during retirement?

- What is my time frame? When do I need to start taking income from my plan?

- What strategy do I have in place to do so now?

- How much Social Security will I get?

- Do I have a pension—and what can I expect it to actually pay me when I reach retirement age?

- How do the fees on my investment plan affect my retirement goals?

- If the market cycles again [as it will continue to do as long as Wall Street exists], what steps should I take to protect the money I need to produce for income and basic living expenses?

- Do I have a low volatility investment discipline?

- Do I have any other sources of income (such as rental properties)?

- Have I been making withdrawals from accounts that are intended to be growth investments for retirement income? (You shouldn't be taking income now from a growth portfolio!)

The answers to those questions allow a good financial advisor to build a plan that's tailor-made for the client's individual needs. Then, once that's in place, the advisor and the client continue to review and discuss that plan over the months and years that follow, making any necessary course corrections as they go along.

Inevitably, most of us run into crises in our lives that affect our physical or financial well-being—or both. We don't want these situations to go untreated for very long, because the sooner we take action, the sooner we can get back to health. That's why periodic reviews of both our physical and financial health plans are so essential. When a crisis happens, we want someone who can spot it immediately and then guide us through it. We want someone who is able to tell us exactly what to do to address the problem.

Imagine that the next time you visit your doctor he decides you need an operation and refers you to a surgeon. You don't want the surgeon to take a quick look at you, schedule your surgery, and then hand you the same pamphlet she hands out to everyone who comes into her office. No, you want her to sit down with you for a pre-op consultation. You want her to order all the tests she needs—blood work, CAT scans, chest X-rays, etc.—so she can be fully aware of your exact state of health before the surgery. And then you want her to explain precisely what she's going to do and why—and what you can expect after the surgery. Once the surgery is done, you wouldn't be very happy if the surgeon signed off on you and scheduled a follow-up appointment for five years down the road. Instead, you'd expect a post-op visit, where the surgeon checks on your response to the surgery. She tells you what to watch for, what you can and can't do, and how you can maintain and support the healing process, and she probably sets up a schedule for ongoing visits either with her or your primary care physician.

Most of us know what to expect of a good surgeon. We'd feel pretty nervous going under the knife if we didn't have absolute confidence in that expert. But many times folks don't know that they should feel just as uneasy about a financial advisor who takes their money, hands them a folder full of pie charts and glossy marketing materials, and says goodbye. To me, that's almost as scary—and irresponsible—as a surgeon who didn't provide you with adequate before-and-after consultation and reviews.

Just as your physical body is one of a kind, so is your financial situation. A cookie-cutter financial plan is nearly as dangerous to your well-being as cookie-cutter health care would be.

YOUR PLAYBOOK FOR THE FUTURE

As we discussed earlier, none of us has any control over international politics and the world economy. Just as the political scene in the 1990s had repercussions for the markets and my family, political and economic challenges in Europe today worry investors and have a ripple effect all over the world. The same sort of ups and downs will keep happening, and there is little we can do to predict them, just like we can't predict when a personal crisis might change our financial circumstances. The best we can do is plan for the worst so that if it happens it doesn't catch us unprepared.

Some things, however, we *can* predict. For example, we all know that the day will come when we'll have to retire—and yet a lot of people don't think much about it when they're in their thirties and forties (or even fifties). Then, when they realize that retirement is only five or so years away, they start to get uneasy. If they're not careful, they wake up one day and find that retirement is staring them in the face. They're in big trouble if they don't have a financial plan already in place.

Think about a nine-inning baseball game. The head coach has a roster and a strategy—a written plan—for each inning of the game, but the most important one is the final inning. That's when he'll bring in his closer to shut down the other team's offense and seal their victory. He's got it all planned out before the umpire yells "Play ball!" In fact, the coach probably has a couple of pitching scenarios worked out for the end of the game—just in case the situation changes. He can't predict those circumstances exactly, but he can map out some likely scenarios and have a plan in place that covers them all. What's more, he doesn't just have a few ideas tucked away inside his head; he'll have done his homework ahead of time, taken notes, and written out each step of the way.

That's what you need for a good retirement plan: a written, detailed plan that contains your income strategies for retirement (including the possibility that retirement comes a lot sooner than you expect). Your trusted advisors are the people to help you make this plan. They can figure out exactly what payment options you have from Social Security and other income sources, and then they can help you determine how much income you'll need to generate from your portfolios—and how you can do that in the most efficient way. With your advisors' help, you can structure a plan that's both solid enough and flexible enough to get you though whatever comes up in life. Having a financial plan won't take away the emotional pain of a sudden crisis, but at least the trauma won't be compounded by not having enough money to cope with it.

FINDING THE RIGHT PATH

Much like a baseball coach with his lineup and pitching rotation, when I sit down with a client I know that my responsibility is to make sure that individual has a well-thought-out plan in place that will cover anything that might come up. I put it in writing because I want to be sure that we're both clear on every step that lies ahead. I'm well aware that in today's world, all kinds of things can mean we'll have to adjust the client's financial plan, and I take all of them into consideration. Obviously, no one can keep those things from happening, but I *can* make sure that there's a plan in place if they do happen.

We've talked a lot about how a personal crisis can affect your finances, and we've also discussed the role the overall economy will play in your financial future. These are definitely two of the important factors I consider each time I create a financial plan. But there are also other factors I know are at play today, some serious curveballs that will require serious thought to come out ahead in retirement.

A PENSION-LESS SOCIETY

One of these is the fact that we're becoming a pension-less society. Where once many workers could count on a retirement income from their employers, now more and more corporations are doing away with their pension plans. Many times, these companies have no choice. An aging workforce and failing businesses have overloaded the system, and there is simply not enough money left in the pension funds to cover everyone who was enrolled. This means that many people are suddenly discovering that the income they were counting on in their retirement years will be a lot less than they had expected.

That's a major recalculation that has to be made—and the sooner they can make it, the better off they will be when it comes time for them to retire.

Baby boomers are likely to be the last generation to receive any sort of lifetime check from employer pensions. The folks who are trailing along behind the boomers—and every generation that comes after them—are going to have to rely on proper planning if they want retirement security. Financial advisors like me will have an important role providing hands-on education for these younger generations. Retirement planning is going to be a necessary fact of life for almost everyone, and the younger they can begin, the more secure their futures will be.

GOOD NEWS / BAD NEWS

Here's the good news: people are living longer today than ever before, and they're also staying healthy and active longer. Now the bad news: well, it's exactly the same as the good news! People are living longer today than ever before, and they're also staying healthy and active longer. How can this be bad news? Because it's a major reason why many people are having to reconsider their financial journey to retirement.

Modern medicine and technology have changed our average life span. Odds are good that in the near future we're going to see even more cures discovered and new surgeries and procedures invented that will extend the lives of many people who would otherwise have died. The insurance world (both life and health) is aware of this trend, and insurance companies are changing their rates accordingly.

It's a major change in our world, and it has far-reaching economic implications at both the personal and national levels.

Financial advisors used to refer to what they called the "4 percent rule." This rule of thumb for retirement planning said that if you withdrew 4 percent of your portfolio each year during retirement, you'd have enough money to last three decades. Well, that sounds pretty good, doesn't it? But let's say you retire at fifty-nine, which was the average retirement age back in 2004.[1] That means you have enough money to last you until you're eighty-nine. But what if you were to live well into your nineties? That's not all that unusual today, and more and more people are even living past one hundred. You don't want to outlive your retirement income by ten years or more!

Imagine as you boarded an airplane flying from New York City to Tampa, Florida, a distance of about a thousand miles, the flight attendant told you, "I'm afraid we may not have enough fuel to make it the entire distance. But don't worry. We can get you at least 890 miles into your journey. Then we'll probably need to let you off in Atlanta, Georgia."

"But how am I going to get from Atlanta to Tampa?" you ask her. "I have to be in Tampa by tonight."

"Well," she'd say, "you're on your own once we land in Atlanta. We can't help you. I'm sure you'll figure out something."

I don't know about you, but I'd get off that airplane pretty fast! And I feel the same way about any retirement plan that only gets my client to their eighty-ninth birthday. These days, that's just not long enough. It doesn't cover the entire retirement journey.

1 Rebecca Riffkin, "Average US Retirement Age Rises to 62," Gallup, April 28, 2014, http://www.gallup.com/poll/168707/average-retirement-age-rises.aspx.

RECALCULATING YOUR RETIREMENT PLAN BASED ON TODAY'S ECONOMY

Another reason you may need to recalculate your financial plan has to do with changes in our overall economy. It's also another reason why the 4 percent rule no longer works.

A California financial advisor named William Bengen came up with the 4 percent rule in the early 1990s.[2] He said that if you had a balanced portfolio—invested in 55 to 60 percent stocks and 40 to 45 percent bonds—you could withdraw that 4 percent per year we mentioned earlier, and it would last throughout your retirement. Well, it was a beautiful idea while it lasted. It gave people a mathematical formula they could rely on for determining a strong retirement plan. But like we've already said, retirement plans need to be both strong and flexible. No math equation can ever cover all the economic variables of the twenty-first century.

The reason why the 4 percent rule no longer works isn't only because people are living longer. It also no longer works in today's economic reality. A recent article in *The Wall Street Journal* had this to say:

> *If you had retired Jan. 1, 2000, with an initial 4% with-drawal rate and a portfolio of 55% stocks and 45% bonds rebalanced each month, with the first year's withdrawal amount increased by 3% a year for inflation, your portfolio would have fallen by a third through 2010, according to investment firm T. Rowe Price Group. And you would be left*

---

2 William Bengen, "Determining Withdrawal Rates Using Historical Data," *Journal of Financial Planning*, October 1994, http://www.retailinvestor.org/pdf/Bengen1.pdf.

with only a 29% chance of making it through three decades,
the firm estimates.[3]

To say this another way, if you retire when you are sixty and you live to be ninety, you have a 71 percent chance of running out of money. The rule no longer works. If financial advisors continue to rely on it in our current economy, lots of folks will end up with a financial plan that's too flimsy to hold up. It's bound to break. We can't avoid getting old—but broke and old are two things most of us would not like to experience together!

Why is our economic reality so different than, say, twenty years ago? Well, there are a bunch of factors at work, such as the wars and military conflicts in different parts of the world. We also have a different kind of war going on—a war on saving. We've been living for years in a world of globally suppressed interest rates. When savings accounts are offering interest rates that are less than 1 percent (in fact, many of them are not much more than 0 percent),[4] people are moving into riskier investment territories to find the returns they need on their money. That's not a good answer, though. You need a financial advisor who can help you adjust to the new economic reality in creative ways that don't put your hard-earned money at risk. One way that we will discuss more is using a low volatility investment discipline that will both avoid large losses and manage your exposure to risk. These plans yield smaller, more incremental returns but help to protect your investments from large losses that can decimate your nest egg. As you will see, I stress-test your portfolio with this phi-

3 Kelly Greene, "Say Goodbye to the 4% Rule," *The Wall Street Journal,* March 3, 2013, http://www.wsj.com/articles/SB10001424127887324162304578304491492559684.

4 Paul Sisolak, "The 10 Best Savings Accounts in 2016," *US News & World Report,* January 21, 2016, http://money.usnews.com/money/blogs/my-money/articles/2016-01-21/the-10-best-savings-accounts-of-2016.

losophy in mind to create sustainable income with an optimized risk management plan in place to keep your savings growing responsibly into retirement.

REGULAR CHECKUPS

Much like your body as it ages, your portfolio needs the same sort of extra attention as you near retirement. As the years go by, the odds increase that something could throw your financial plan off course—and if you've done it right, there's going to be a lot of money in there that could be affected. At the same time, you don't have as much time to make those course adjustments, so an early response is urgent.

At my firm, we do something we call "stress tests." We're not testing our clients' hearts, of course; instead, we're testing the health of our clients' portfolios. We look at more than twenty-five factors to uncover risks our clients may not have been aware of (such as the effects of defense spending or the rise and fall of interest rates). We also discover undisclosed and hidden fees they never knew were lurking inside their portfolios. We look for stock intersections and overlaps; we find out how diversified their portfolios truly are.

This isn't a one-time thing. We give our clients a portfolio stress test at least twice a year, especially when they're at the point in their lives where they're seeking to generate a cash flow from their investments. This brings to light anything that could be causing a decline in their portfolio at such a crucial time in their lives—and allows us to take immediate action.

I want to make sure my clients won't ever run out of money during their retirement years, that they won't outlive their financial plan, and that they'll be in good shape to weather all of life's ups and downs. I don't want them to ever face the sort of nasty surprise my parents did when they discovered they didn't have the resources to maintain their lifestyle.

When I give my clients the financial stress test, sometimes we discover that they're in pretty good shape, and they'll only need an extra $100 a month to get them where they need to be. Other folks, though, are going to need $1,000 a month. Each circumstance will need a different set of strategies. Everyone's situation is different. The lifestyle they want, the amounts of income they'll need to achieve that, and the income streams they already have in place will all be unique to each of them.

WHAT'S YOUR NUMBER?

You can't have a one-size-fits-all retirement plan, because there's no single answer to the question of how much you need to retire. And it's a hard number to come up with by yourself. I usually spend some time working with my clients to determine all the expenses they'll be facing in their retirement years.

Here are some of the expenses on the list:

- mortgage or rental costs

- home maintenance

- transportation (gasoline costs or public transportation fares)

- auto maintenance

- food (including eating out)

- utilities (including trash pickup, cable, Internet connection, etc., as well as heat, electricity, and phone)

- medical prescriptions

- doctor's visits

- insurance payments (property, auto, health, and life)

- clothing

- entertainment

- hobbies

- pets (veterinarian bills, for example, or boarding and grooming fees)

- taxes

- inflation/cost of living increases

- vacation and travel

- holidays (such as Christmas, Hanukkah, etc.)

- birthdays

- gifts

- books and magazines

- periodic expenses (things you only pay once or twice a year)

- an emergency "bucket" (for all the things that *might* come up; if you never have to use it, that's great, but at least you'll have the peace of mind of knowing it's there if you should need it)

- discretionary spending

Some of the things on that list are more obvious than others. Almost everyone, though, finds that there are at least several expenses they've never considered before when they've planned for their retirement needs. (One of the big ones I run into is that people never seem to count the money they hand out to their grandkids whenever they see them. It may be just a few dollars at a time—but that money has to come from somewhere.) As my clients and I work through a very precise budget sheet, sooner or later they always say, "I didn't think of that. . . Yeah, you're right. I never calculated that expense, at least not on paper."

You need to learn what it could really take to maintain your lifestyle during retirement. Can you *really* know? Probably not, but you can get a much better idea if you ask yourself more in-depth questions. For example:

- Do you plan to stay in the same home you're living in now?

- Is that home paid off?

- Is it in good repair? Can you expect it to stay in good repair for the years to come? Even if your house is in great shape now, it will need upkeep as it ages. Depending on where you live, there are a number of potential future issues you may want to prepare for, such as water or storm damage, tree trimming and grounds maintenance, and replacement of your roof, air conditioner, or water heater down the road.

- What about your utilities? You may have a good feel for how much you're paying for them now, but will that number be the same once you've retired and are spending more time at home? And you'll want to make sure you're accounting for inflation. How much will that same utility usage look like ten, twenty, or thirty years from now? Depending on our fuel sources and availability, home utilities could surpass the typical inflation rates.

All this may seem like information that's fairly straightforward and obvious. I've found, though, that it's easy to overlook things that only seem obvious after they've been drawn to your attention. When people see the numbers written down on paper, they get a better picture of where their money goes. And if it's obvious that their retirement income isn't going to cover the expenses they take for granted, they have a good tool for evaluating what will need to change. Some folks say, for example, "Look at our cable bill. That's crazy. We don't need to pay that much when most of the time we only watch Netflix anyway." Or they might say, "I never realized how much money we spend eating out." They'll look at each other and say, "Honey, just think how much money we could have been saving if we had looked at this sooner!"

Don't think of a budget as something that will restrict you. Actually, the more information you have about your finances, the more freedom you have. Those budget numbers allow folks to evaluate what's truly most important in their lives. They can decide, for instance, that they'd far rather save up for a yearly vacation trip than spend so much money on eating out several times a week. Or they might realize that if they stopped handing out five-dollar bills every time they saw their grandchildren, they could afford to give them more substantial birthday and Christmas gifts.

I also find that a lot of folks haven't prepared for unexpected health expenses, nor have they acknowledged that their health expenses are likely to increase during their retirement years. People say to me, "I've been healthy my whole life. I barely use the health insurance I get through my employer—so once I have to pay for my insurance myself after I retire, it seems like a waste of money to pay so much for something I never use. I'd rather just wait for Medicare to kick in and take my chances." Well, guess what? Some folks have never gotten into a car accident in thirty or forty years of driving—but it only takes once to make their car insurance payments well worth their money. So unless you like living dangerously, health insurance is one of your best financial investments. (And if you do like to gamble with your future, I'd recommend you go to Las Vegas instead.)

AVOID SWISS ARMY KNIVES

Swiss Army knives are an amazing invention. They do a lot of things, but everything they do is in a small capacity. They have a tiny little saw, for example, which will come in handy if you need to cut up sticks—but won't do you any good at all if you want to chop down a tree. Swiss Army knives also have scissors you can use to snip through small bits of fabric or whatever—but you won't be cutting up any large bolts of cloth. These knives are pretty clever, but they're just not designed to handle big jobs.

And that's not what your retirement plan should look like. Yes, you want it to have its own special functions and strategies for each of your financial needs. But variety alone isn't going to ensure your future. You need strategies that are big enough to truly make a difference, that have the capability to handle even life's largest challenges. You want to be able to face the future with confidence, without the anxiety and stress that comes from worrying that you might run short during your retirement years.

Retirement will represent a fundamental shift in your life. Your retirement strategy should allow that shift to take place. As you retire from the phase of your life where you worked and earned, you want your money to also retire from its growth phase. This is the time in your life when you want to be able to relax and enjoy life without any work worries—and it's time for your hard-earned money to allow you to fully enjoy the fruits of all your labors.

Adjusting to retirement is emotionally difficult for most people—and worries about money will only make it more so—but there may be strategies and products that many advisors overlook that could significantly help your situation. I can't guarantee what the future returns on your investments will be, and I certainly don't know the date of your death—but I *can* help you create a plan that will put your mind at rest, no matter what the future holds.

Here's an example of the sort of plan I like to know my clients have. I helped this particular man achieve retirement savings of $1 million. Based on his age and the makeup of his portfolio, the percentage of his withdrawals is 4.5 percent. That means he's taking out $45,000 annually, which with his Social Security payments is enough to cover his needs. I've set things up so that the amount he withdraws from his portfolio can never go below $45,000, regardless of the performance of his investments. If the $1 million is reduced by 10 percent, he still receives $45,000. However, if the portfolio increases by 10 percent, his new income would be $49,500. With this, his new base is increased, and now that can never be reduced.

I also try to help every new client who comes in with an IRA or 401(k)—what's called "qualified money"—to avoid the Swiss Army knives. The client usually knows that after age fifty-nine and a half he can access the money without the 10 percent penalty. What many clients don't know is that by the age of seventy and a half, they must take out what's called the required minimum distribution (RMD). If it's not taken by a certain time, they can be penalized up to 50 percent of their entire portfolio. So I work with my client to create a financial plan that includes not only how but also when he can access the income he needs during retirement. Many new clients also believe that they must take all of the stated RMD. That is false. We help educate them about how to strategically set up their RMD strategy so that if they don't want or need additional income and taxes we can relieve them of that to a certain percent.

These are just a few simple scenarios to show why you need a trusted advisor who can help you create the retirement plan you need. Most everything in life goes more smoothly when there's a plan in place ahead of time, and retirement is no exception.

It may seem like a daunting task to make that plan. At first glance, many people feel overwhelmed. After all, no one knows exactly how long they'll need to plan for. Even with the statistics available about life expectancy, plenty of people live a few years longer and sometimes a decade past their predicted life expectancy. How do you find the balance between making sure that you're covered financially in the case that you surpass expectations and having a reliable income to spend day to day in the years between? Can you live the lifestyle you deserve and spend with confidence over the duration of your retirement?

Sometimes people just don't want to face these questions. Those are probably the same folks who avoid going to the doctor because they're afraid they'll hear bad news. It's a normal human tendency to want to put our heads in the sand. We're a lot like little kids, hiding under the covers because we think that if we can't see something, it can't hurt us. Many pre-retirees are apprehensive about taking a close, hard look at their future expenses and income for fear it might look like bad news. They also don't want to face the reality of old age.

But like I said before—facing the facts gives you more control over life, not less. And the news won't necessarily be bad! When you sit down with an advisor to make a plan, you might be pleasantly surprised by what your money can do for you.

AN UNDEFEATED SEASON

The way I've always seen it is that by the time you reach retirement, you've *already* won the game of life. You don't want to jeopardize that now. Instead, you want a plan that will ensure that you keep enjoying it.

That's what I want my clients to achieve, and that's why I'm writing this book. If you're not confident that your advisor has created a plan to ensure you can enjoy a streak of wins, you might need to get a different coach. At the very least, you should get a second opinion.

CHAPTER 3

COMMON RETIREMENT MISTAKES

R ight now, the largest generation of retirees in our nation's history is entering their retirement years following the worst economic downturn since the Great Depression. When you think about it, the timing couldn't be worse for baby boomers, who are beset with a host of retirement challenges. Combine these factors with their longer life expectancy and the fact that many don't have a solid financial plan, and the difficulties increase. When it comes to planning for their retirement, they don't have room to make mistakes.

I know that retirement mistakes can cause catastrophic hardship. That's why I want to warn you about some of the most common mistakes before you make them.

MISTAKE 1: NOT HAVING A STRATEGY

According to a recent study conducted by Wells Fargo, 41 percent of middle-class Americans between the ages of fifty and fifty-nine are not currently saving for retirement. Nearly a third of the people in the study said they will not have enough money to "survive" retirement, while 19 percent of all respondents have *no* retirement savings.[5] According to the Retirement Confidence Survey from the Employee Benefits Research Institute, 48 percent of workers haven't even calculated how much money they need to save for retirement.[6] This worries me a lot.

Our grandparents probably didn't have much of a retirement strategy. They didn't need one. As we discussed in chapter 2, not having a written retirement plan today is like saying you're going to cross the United States on foot without a map or GPS. The retirement programs our grandparents counted on are no longer the certain things they once were. These days, we can't assume that someone else will take care of us once we retire. We have to actively take responsibility for our own retirement incomes.

Not everyone agrees that Social Security is in danger, but there are indications that we should at least be prepared for this retirement staple to eventually fail. According to a 2005 report made by Stephen C. Goss, chief actuary of the Social Security Administration, to the House Ways and Means Committee, the ratio of covered workers versus the number of beneficiaries under the US Social Security program has gone down quite a bit over the years. In 1940, there

5   "Wells Fargo Survey Finds Saving for Retirement Not Happening for a Third of Middle Class," Wells Fargo, October 22, 2014, https://www.wellsfargo.com/about/press/2014/middle-class-retirement-saving_1022.

6 Retirement Confidence Survey, Employer Benefit Research Institute, 2015, https://www.ebri.org/surveys/rcs/.

were 35.3 million workers paying into the system, with only 222,000 beneficiaries (in other words, there were 159 workers contributing to the system for every single beneficiary collecting from it). By 2003, the number of workers had increased to 154.3 million, with 46.8 million beneficiaries (only 3.3 workers for every single beneficiary). Goss said:

> *In the 2005 Trustees Report, the intermediate projections indicate that the annual excess of tax income over program cost will begin to decline in 2009, and in 2017 cost will exceed tax income. At that point the accumulated trust fund assets of about $2.4 trillion in present value will begin to be used to augment tax income so that benefits scheduled in current law will continue to be paid in full. These assets are, by law, invested wholly in securities backed by the full faith and credit of the United States Government, and have always been redeemed when needed. While there is no question that these securities will be redeemed when needed, this redemption will require the Federal Government to increase taxes, lower other expenditures, or issue publicly-held debt in amounts equal to the net redemptions by the trust funds.*
>
> *If no changes are made, it is projected that the combined trust fund assets would become exhausted in 2041 and the program would no longer be considered to be solvent. This means that we would no longer be able to fully pay benefits scheduled in current law on a timely basis. Instead, we would be able to provide 74 percent of scheduled benefits with continuing tax revenues. After 2041, program cost is projected to continue growing faster than tax income. By 2079, 68*

percent of scheduled benefits are expected to be payable if no changes are made.[7]

Private pension plans are in trouble, too. As we mentioned in the last chapter, it used to be that many Americans had a pension that was provided by their company or government employer. The company would pay a regular amount, usually a portion of that employee's salary while they were employed, every month from retirement until the end of their life. Of course, when this practice was begun, life expectancies were much shorter—which meant that fewer people were drawing from the pension funds at the same time. Today, things are very different. Companies can't afford to give their employees pensions, and existing pensions are slowly disappearing.

According to the Bureau of Labor Statistics, these days only 22 percent of private-sector American workers have a pension set up for them; back in 1990, the percentage was 42, so things have changed a lot over the past thirty years or so. Those who do have a pension might not be able to rely on it lasting through their whole retirement, as the country's financial landscape remains unpredictable.

In 2014, the *Washington Post* reported that the US government was taking steps "that would for the first time allow the benefits of current retirees to be severely cut . . . part of an effort to save some of the nation's most distressed pension plans." The article went on to say:

> *As many as 200 multi-employer plans covering 1.5 million workers are in danger of running out of money over the next two decades. Half of those are thought to be in such bad*

---

7 Stephen C. Goss, Testimony for the House Ways and Means Subcommittee on Social Security, May 24, 2005, https://www.ssa.gov/legislation/testimony_052405.html.

shape that they could seek pension reductions for retirees in the near future.... The idea of cutting benefits is reluctantly supported by some unions and retirement fund managers who see it as the only way to salvage pensions in plans that are in imminent danger of running out of money.[8]

Along the same lines, CNBC reported:

Both public and private pension funds were hit hard by the 2008 financial crisis, which wiped out trillions of investments used to pay retiree benefits... Declining union enrollments, for example, mean there are fewer active workers to cover the cost benefits for retirees, many of whom are living longer than was expected when these plans were established. Multi-employer plans also face the added burden of their pooled pension liabilities. When one member of the plan fails to keep up with contributions, for example, the burden on the other members increases. In the last four years, the Department of Labor has notified workers in more than 600 of these plans that their plans are in "critical or endangered status."[9]

There have been companies that looked too big to fail ten, fifteen, or twenty years ago that went bankrupt and were unable to fulfill their obligations to provide a pension to their former employees. Other companies are offering a one-time lump-sum buyout of employee pensions in order to reduce or eliminate this liability. Forewarned is forearmed. Be prepared for the fact that your pension might not be

8 Michael A. Fletcher, "Congressional Leaders Hammer Out Deal to Allow Pension Plans to Cut Retiree Benefits," *Washington Post*, December 9, 2014.

9 John W. Schoen, "Congress Eyes Move to Cut Pension Benefits," CNBC, December 10, 2014, http://www.cnbc.com/2014/12/10/congress-eyes-move-to-cut-pension-benefits.html.

as much as you were expecting—or that it might not be there at all someday. This is just one reason why having a personal strategy will be more critical to your financial confidence in retirement than it was to the generations that came before you. By taking a proactive approach to the retirement savings that you control, you can plan for the worst-case scenario—your pension being eliminated—and still be prepared for retirement.

MISTAKE 2: NOT KNOWING YOUR RETIREMENT EXPENSES

What are the things you'll truly *need* during retirement? I'm talking about things like housing, food, and health care. Now think about the things you *want* during your retirement. This could be traveling, a hobby, or a certain level of lifestyle. So many people don't realize that you need to plan for both. Many new retirees will take a few trips they have been meaning to take, make some updates to their house, and then quickly realize how fast their bank account is decreasing because they just assumed they would "figure it out later." It's a dangerous mistake.

You also need to keep in mind the increasing medical costs associated with age. This problem is compounded by the fact that not only will you be facing future inflation in this area also but you will also be less able to return to work if you end up running short of money.

Typically, as we age, our bodies need an increasing amount of care. When you retire, you're likely to be in better health than you will be in a decade or two (or three) down the line. You could have additional health-care expenses from what you have now because of more frequent doctor office visits, new medications, surgery, or home health care. You may eventually need to live in an assisted-care facility, which is very costly. What's more, as you grow older and your assistance needs increase, it will get even more expensive.

Back in chapter 2, we already began discussing the expenses you'll have during retirement, but you also need to keep in mind that the cost of certain activities—activities that may seem like optional recreation or leisure pastimes—could actually be essential to your well-being during your retirement. Human beings are kept at our healthiest and happiest by continuing to regularly engage in activities after retirement. Scientists have found that older adults who stay physically active have improved mental and physical health, and they're more likely to remain sharp intellectually.[10] Furthermore, challenging or difficult activities can provide us with the greatest benefit in this regard. A recent study reported that:

> *Older adults and seniors benefit by learning new skills; the more challenging the skills learned by older adults, the better it is for overall brain health and cognition. Being mentally active requires more than just being a spectator; being mentally active involves participating in a challenging mental activity.[11]*

When we're obligated to participate in these sorts of activities as part of jobs during our working years, we often overlook the fact that they

10 Patrick D. Gajewski and Michael Falkenstein, "Physical Activity and Neurocognitive Functioning in Aging—A Condensed Updated Review," *European Review of Aging and Physical Activity*, 2016, 13:1, DOI: 10.1186/s11556-016-0161-3.

11 "Learning New Technology Benefits Health of Seniors," *Orlando Sentinel*, June 24, 2014, http://articles.orlandosentinel.com/2014-06-24/classified/os-learning-new-technology-benefits-health-of-seniors-20140624_1_new-technology-older-adults-activity.

have benefits aside from bringing in money. Regardless of whether or not you enjoyed your career, you may be surprised to find out just how much it was doing to keep you in good repair!

When you were working, those activities that helped keep you in good health were also providing you income. Once you retire, the tables will flip: instead of getting paid for being active, you will be paying for the privilege. From gym memberships to art classes, from museum memberships to the various clubs that you may be interested in joining, these "leisure" activities should never be considered frivolous or unnecessary to your well-being. In fact, studies have found that older adults who take their leisure activities seriously—who commit to them as an ongoing way of life—are the ones who are the happiest and healthiest.[12]

So when you calculate your expenses during retirement, don't overlook the things that today you may consider optional recreational activities. During retirement, these will be vital to your overall health.

MISTAKE 3: UNDERESTIMATING YOUR LONGEVITY

Everyone knows that life expectancies for children born today are very different from the life expectancies for children born a century ago. But even that isn't the whole picture. As we said, your life expectancy also changes, depending on how old you are.

Of course, statistics like the tables we've discussed earlier only give us the average numbers for longevity. And not everyone even

12 Junhyoung Kim et al, "Health Benefits of Serious Involvement in Leisure Activities Among Older Korean Adults," *International Journal of Qualitative Studies on Health and Well-being*, 2014, 9:10, 10.3402/qhw.v9.24616 PMCID: PMC4110381.

agrees these are accurate numbers. Researchers from the International Monetary Fund have shown that forecasters have consistently underestimated how long people will live by an average of three years.[13] Add to that the accelerating progress of technology and medical research, and you can see that many people are likely to live longer than many of the tables suggest.

Ultimately, no table can tell us how long we'll live. Your expiration date could be sooner or more distant than predicted. People have been known to beat the odds! Ida May Fuller, the first person to receive a Social Security check, is a good example.

Ida May retired in November 1939 from her job as a legal secretary, and she started collecting benefits in January 1940 when she was sixty-five. When Ida May was born in 1874, a baby girl was predicted to live to around age forty-five,[14] so by the time she retired, Ida May had already beaten the averages—and then she went on to live to be one hundred years old.[15]

Ida May's story is just another example of the reality that regardless of the age you were projected to live to when you were born, you could far surpass that age, especially as medical advances are constantly being made. According to Aubrey de Grey, a researcher in gerontology, the first person who will live to be 150 has already been

13 Frances Denmark, "Life, Death, & the Numbers," *Institutional Investor*, September 2014, http://www.cenveomobile.com/i/378619-sept-2014/84.

14 "Life Expectancy Graphs: 1850–2000." Mapping History, http://mappinghistory.uoregon.edu/english/US/US39-0 l.html. (Accessed January 6, 2015.)

15 Larry DeWitt (compiler), "Research Note #3: Details of Ida May Fuller's Payroll Tax Contributions," Social Security Administration: Agency History, July 1996, http://www.ssa.gov/history/idapayroll.html.

born.[16] That person may not be you, but it's still worth your time and effort to prepare financially for a very long life.

MISTAKE 4: USING "OLD ECONOMY" RULES IN TODAY'S ECONOMY

As I mentioned earlier, retirees were once advised to take out about 4 percent of their total portfolio amount per year. With today's higher cost of living, however, they might actually have to take as much as 5 percent per year, but even if that weren't the case, the 4 percent rule still wouldn't work in today's economic reality. That's because it was calculated using very different numbers from those that exist today.

As you can see from the following chart, some of the greatest gains in US stock market history were between 1980 and 1999. With market increases like that, withdrawing 4 percent per year was a pretty good idea. But we can't base our saving behavior today on what worked in the previous century. The stock market is in a different pattern today.

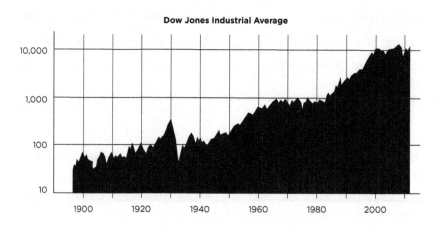

Dow Jones Industrial Average

16 John Nosta, "The First Person to Live to 150 Has Already Been Born—Revisited!" *Forbes*, February 3, 2013.

We talked about this already in chapter 2, but it's an important issue that can't be discussed enough. Many analysts think that people who use the 4 percent rule in today's market scenario still have a 90 percent chance of having enough money to last their lifetimes.[17] That may sound good, but I don't like those odds.

When we talked about this earlier, I compared the problem to a flight from New York City to Tampa that could only get you as far as Atlanta. This time, I want you to imagine you board a plane that has about a hundred passengers taking the flight. You get on, find your seat, and settle down with your magazine. As the plane prepares for takeoff, the flight attendant begins her safety instruction speech. You've heard it all before, so you're barely listening—until she says something that makes you look up and pay attention.

"Ladies and gentlemen, I want to assure you this is a very safe flight. In fact, we've determined that you have a 90 percent chance of arriving at your destination safely."

How do you like those odds now? Would you want to be on a flight that had a 10 percent chance of crashing?

It's no better if the flight attendant says instead, "This is a very safe flight. In fact, even if we do have to make an emergency landing, 90 percent of you will probably live." In other words, ten people on the plane would die in the event of an emergency landing. I doubt many people would want to stay on the plane—but that's the kind of risk you're facing if your advisor is using the 4 percent rule to determine how much income you'll need during retirement.

---

17 Rob Williams, "Is the 4% Rule Still Appropriate?" Charles Schwab, August 5, 2014, http://www.schwab.com/public/schwab/nn/articles/Is-the-4-Percent-Rule-Still-Appropriate.

Using these "old economy" concepts hurt a lot of people in 2008 when the stock market suffered a dramatic loss during the housing crash of 2008. The basic wisdom that the market always recovers after its big losses held true when you consider the long-term perspective: investors *did* eventually recoup what they had lost—that is, so long as they didn't withdraw funds during the 2008 crisis. For those who needed to take income from their investments, the volatility of the time caused a lot more damage. Those retirees may have never been able to fully recover financially.

How likely is this to happen to you during your retirement? Well, historically, market corrections occur on average every five to seven years. This means you could experience losses five or even six times during your retirement. During those market downturns, would you be able to maintain your lifestyle?

I'm not saying you should never invest in the stock market. I just want you to be sure to set yourself up so that you never have to change your lifestyle because of market fluctuations.

MISTAKE 5: NOT BEING STRATEGIC ABOUT TAXES

You've heard the saying "Nothing is certain except death and taxes." Well, it's true that paying taxes is inevitable. But there are steps you can take that will ensure you pay less tax. You can structure your retirement so that it's more tax efficient and potentially keep more of your hard-earned money for retirement.

TAX DEFERRED

Tax-deferred accounts, like traditional IRAs, give you immediate tax deductions on the full amount of whatever you contribute to them. Then, down the road, when you take money out of those accounts during retirement, your withdrawals from the account will be taxed. For example, if your taxable income this year is $100,000 and you contributed $5,000 to a tax-deferred account, you would only pay tax this year on $95,000 rather than $100,000. Now let's say that after you retire you start out with a total income of $45,000, based on your pension and Social Security payments. If you take out $5,000 from your tax-deferred account, your taxable income that year will be bumped up to $50,000.

So you're going to have to pay taxes sooner or later on that money—but by shifting when you pay them, you can take advantage of tax-free investment growth. Also, you may be in a lower tax bracket after you retire, which would mean that same $5,000 would be taxed at a lower percentage rate than it would be now. I'll show you how this works out. Let's say you are paying a 25 percent tax rate on your income now. If you contribute $2,000 to a tax-deferred account, that will give you an additional tax refund of $500 (0.25 x $2,000), which means you'll have that much more to put into your retirement savings. (In other words, it gives you the double advantage of saving your taxes now, while also increasing the amount you have available to save.) Then when it comes time for you to withdraw that $2,000, you're in the 15 percent tax bracket, so you will only pay $300 in taxes on it.

TAX EXEMPT

Tax-exempt accounts, on the other hand, give you tax benefits down the road when you take out the money. Contributions into the account are made with after-tax dollars, so there's no immediate tax advantage—*but* your investment grows tax-free. A Roth IRA is a popular investment vehicle for this. The advantage of these accounts is usually seen with younger investors. If you're early in your career, you're probably in a lower tax bracket than you will be later—and when it comes time to withdraw the money, it won't push you into a higher bracket, because you won't have to pay any additional taxes on it. Even the interest on these accounts is untaxed. In other words, if over the course of twenty-five years you put $5,000 a year into a tax-exempt account with 7 percent interest, by the time you retired at sixty-five, you would have accumulated more than $338,000 in the account. You will already have paid taxes on $125,000 of that amount, but you'll never have to pay taxes on the $213,000 you received in interest. Ultimately, whenever you have an investment that will grow significantly over time, you're probably going to be better off keeping it in a tax-exempt account.

WHICH IS RIGHT FOR YOU?

Usually the most efficient tax strategy maximizes contributions to both tax-deferred and taxed-exempt accounts. Lower-income earners should probably focus on funding a tax-exempt fund, while higher earners will see more benefits from tax-deferred accounts. Here are some of your options (which you should discuss with your trusted financial advisor):

- **Mutual Funds:** These distribute capital gains annually to all shareholders, regardless of whether those investors have actually liquidated any of their shares or not. Government and corporate bonds pay regular interest that is federally taxable, unless it is paid into a tax-deferred account of some sort. Most interest and dividend income is taxed at the same rate as IRA and retirement-plan distributions, but in some cases it can actually be taxed at a lower rate.

- **Taxable Investments:** Some types of investments grow with fairly good efficiency even though they are taxable. In general, any investment or security that qualifies for capital gains treatment is a good candidate for a taxable savings account. This includes individual equities, hard assets (such as real estate and precious metals), and certain types of mutual funds (such as exchange-traded funds and index funds).

- **Stocks:** Most stocks, particularly those that pay little or nothing in the way of dividends, are better left to grow in a taxable account, as long as they are held for more than a year. Individual stocks that are held in a tax-deferred account can often be taxed at a higher rate than taxable stocks. If the money from stocks' sales is taken as part of a retirement plan, it is taxed as ordinary income.

- **Unit Investment Trusts:** UITs can be useful taxable instruments because when the trust resets at the end of its term any stocks that have lost value can provide deductible capital losses when they are sold. However, investors that actually cash out of their UITs instead of allowing them to reset could face large capital gains distributions.

- **Annuities:** If you own annuities, all earnings are free from income taxes until you start receiving annual payments. (In other words, they are tax-exempt savings vehicles.) Withdrawals of earnings are subject to ordinary income tax, and a 10 percent federal income tax penalty may apply if you take the distribution before you are fifty-nine and a half years old.

SOCIAL SECURITY AND TAXES

Income taxes in retirement can be confusing, especially when it comes to Social Security benefits. If you have other substantial income such as wages, self-employment, interest, dividends, or other taxable income, you likely pay federal income taxes on your Social Security benefits. The current IRS rules are designed to ensure that no one pays federal income tax on more than 85 percent of their Social Security benefits, but some pay far more than others.[18]

For example, when a single retiree's adjusted gross income (plus half of Social Security benefits and any tax-exempt income) exceeds $25,000, only half of the retiree's Social Security benefits are taxable. But if this single retiree's income level rises to over $34,000 (or a couple filing jointly makes at least $32,000 and $44,000), the IRS will tax up to 85 percent of Social Security benefits—the maximum amount. This significant increase in the amount of Social Security benefits taxed is known as the "tax torpedo." It silently creeps up and sinks your savings with a sudden explosion of taxes.

---

18 Internal Revenue Service, "Regular & Disability Benefits," January 1, 2016, https://www.irs.gov/Help-&-Resources/Tools-&-FAQs/FAQs-for-Individuals/Frequently-Asked-Tax-Questions-&-Answers/Social-Security-Income/Regular-&-Disability-Benefits/Regular-&-Disability-Benefits.

To consider the implications of the tax torpedo, suppose Mary, a single retiree, has $35,000 in income plus her Social Security benefits. She wants to withdraw funds from her 401(k) to pay for an extra $750 of spending that year. Because Mary is in the 25 percent tax bracket, she assumes that she needs to withdraw $1,000 to create $750 of after-tax income.

In reality, this $1,000 withdrawal would cause $850 more of her Social Security benefits to be taxed, increasing her taxable income by $1,850. If you do the math, Mary would pay $462.50 in taxes on the $1,000 withdrawal ($1,850 x 25 percent), putting her in a 46.25 percent marginal tax rate. That is 85 percent higher than her usual 25 percent tax bracket.

If Mary's advisor had let her know she was navigating an income range very close to the tax torpedo, she may have avoided it by withdrawing from her Roth IRA, which would be tax-free. She also could have withdrawn from a taxable account, which might have triggered little or no taxes, rather than her retirement account to finance the additional spending.

A recent study found that the impact of the tax torpedo, while it can be tough on lower-income retirees like Mary, is most dramatic on the nest eggs of retirees in the $250,000-to-$600,000 range. What makes these taxes even worse is that the amounts aren't indexed for inflation, meaning more Social Security benefits are taxed each year due to annual cost-of-living adjustments.

BOTTOM LINE WHEN IT COMES TO TAXES

As you talk over your tax alternatives with your financial advisor, keep in mind that you will *always* pay taxes; it's just a question of when and how much. In order to take full advantage of the various tax alternatives, you must follow very specific tax rules. Work with a qualified retirement planner and certified public accountant who can help you be sure you're following all these necessary rules—and you won't have any nasty tax surprises down the road when you're retired.

MISTAKE 6: NOT ACCOUNTING FOR INFLATION

Much like the explosive tax torpedo, you might think of inflation as "the invisible tax" you will unavoidably have to pay. It is the additional money you have to spend over time for the very same products and services.

Let's say you put money away in a bank savings account that has a 1 percent interest rate. If you deposit $10,000 into your account, after ten years that $10,000 will still be there, plus about $1,046.22 of compounded interest (assuming the interest rate doesn't change in those ten years), so you'll have $11,046.22. At first glance, this can appear to be a relatively "safe" way to invest, even if it doesn't provide enormous gains: you put $10,000 in, and you know that you'll have that same $10,000 when you need it, plus a little bit more. Maybe you didn't gain much, but it looks as though you can at least say you didn't lose anything.

When you factor inflation into this scenario, though, you'll see quite a different picture. Using the years between 2004 and 2014 as an example, let's see what inflation does to your savings' actual buying power. Say you had $10,000 worth of expenses in 2004; because the cost of things increases from year to year, to cover those exact same expenses in 2014 you would have needed $12,569.24. Your "safe" savings account actually lost you $1,523.02 in purchasing power. Since you probably spend a lot more than $10,000 a year, the effects of inflation on your spending will be even greater than what we see in this example.

Unless you strategize ways to overcome the impact of this "invisible tax," inflation can mean your retirement money doesn't go nearly as far as you thought it would. You simply can't use today's costs to predict your income needs ten years down the road. For each passing year, the costs will likely be greater than the years before it. For example, while you may only need $35,000 to sustain yourself and your lifestyle when you are seventy, it could easily turn out that you need $35,700 to maintain that same lifestyle when you are seventy-one. While that might not seem like a huge leap, after ten years the $35,000 you started out needing to cover your expenses will have turned into $42,664.

Looking backward often helps us to look forward more clearly. When we see that prices have steadily gone up over the past century, we can safely project that they will continue to do the same in the decades to come. Take a look at how costs for a few common items have changed in the last forty years (according to the US Census Bureau):

PRODUCT	1975	2015
first-class postage stamp	$0.10	$0.49
gallon of regular gasoline	$0.57	$2.04
gallon of milk	$1.57	$2.69
a dozen eggs	$0.77	$2.88
movie ticket	$2.00	$8.00
average cost of a house	$42,000	$219,600

These are just a few examples, but when you multiply the trend across all your week-to-week and month-to-month purchases year after year, these price increases can begin to take significant bites out of your retirement income. What will your life look like if you're taking the same income per year in the future? The US inflation rate has ranged from minus 15.80 percent to plus 23.70 percent, averaging 3.32 percent over the past one hundred years. Say you hope for the best, and we go with 2 percent as the rate of inflation during your retirement; that means that every $100 you put aside for retirement last year would only be worth $98 next year (in terms of buying power). The year after that, it will be worth $96. After five years, it's worth $90. After ten years, it's worth $80. After twenty years, that initial $100 is now only worth $60 of purchasing power.

Will you still be able to pay all your bills? Will you financially be able to do all the same things you had planned for your retirement? If you compensate by withdrawing more money each year from your portfolio, you'll run into the problem we've already discussed back in chapter 2—you'll run out of money before you run out of life.

MISTAKE 7: NOT DIVERSIFYING YOUR RETIREMENT STRATEGY

Another mistake that investors often make is not diversifying their retirement strategy, or not adjusting it as they age, which can be just as dangerous. By diversifying, you can help protect your principal from unnecessary risk. Whether you invest in less conservative vehicles or more conservative, diversification is important; if one method falls through, another might be successful. You'll also need different strategies at different periods of your life.

TIME IS OF THE ESSENCE

A good retirement portfolio for a thirty-year-old looks different from the retirement portfolio of a sixty-year-old. When you are young, you're in wealth-accumulation mode. At this stage, you may get the most out of your money if you focus on vehicles that emphasize the potential to have significant growth. Typically, with vehicles that offer high gains comes the higher risk that you may face considerable losses. The longer you have between the time when you are investing and the age at which you plan to retire, the greater chance you have of recovering from those losses.

Because of this, as you approach retirement, it's time to shift gears from wealth-accumulation mode to wealth-preservation mode. This shift may not happen all at once; you can do it little by little, so that as you move from one decade to the next, you continue to modify the risk level of the financial vehicles you are using, step by step.

By the time you are ten years away from retirement, a good retirement portfolio is probably focused almost entirely on wealth-preservation vehicles. If you use methods that are too risky in later life, you could lose principal at a time when you don't have the luxury to make it back.

PARTITION YOUR RETIREMENT

You don't need to have the same income source throughout your entire retirement. Instead, you might want to choose one income source for the first ten years or so. (Depending on when you retire, this will be from your late sixties into your midseventies or so.) In today's world, many people are feeling healthy and energetic during this phase of their lives, so this is likely to be an active time, when your expenses may be higher than they will be later on. You may slow down a bit in the next decade (from your midseventies into your mideighties), and so you'll likely be able to live on a lower income. If your retirement lasts thirty or even forty years, you want to be sure you have an income source to cover this period when your health-care costs are likely to go up and you may need long-term care. A good financial plan takes all this into account.

DETERMINE WHY AND WHEN YOU'LL NEED THE MONEY

Choose different savings vehicles for different purposes. You want to ensure that the money you use to pay your bills will be as secure as you can possibly make it. Other expenses—such as entertainment and travel—could come from more risky investments. Vehicles that work well for covering your basic living expenses during retirement will provide you with guaranteed income, principal protection, and enough growth to account for inflation; an annuity would be a good example of this, since annuities may have a lifetime income guarantee as part of the base policy, or you may be able to purchase additional riders to ensure this. Vehicles that work well as sources for nonessential retirement expenses will offer more growth and liquidity because they don't necessarily need to contribute a set amount of income at a regular, specific time.

KEEP SOME ASSETS LIQUID

You may think you have everything covered when it comes to your retirement expenses. But would you have enough on hand if your car was totaled and you had to buy a new one significantly sooner than you had planned? What about if you had an unforeseen medical crisis that required treatments not covered by your insurance? Will you have enough on hand to cover you?

It's a good idea to always have some assets that can be easily liquidated in the event of an emergency. Some investment vehicles may not work as a steady source of income but might be useful in the event of an emergency. Gold is a good example of this kind of asset. Gold isn't a very reliable growth investment—but it's easy to sell when you need extra cash.

USE A VARIETY OF INVESTMENT VEHICLES

Let's talk about some of the pros and cons that go along with various investment vehicles.

Stocks. Among all the investment vehicles out there, stocks can have the greatest growth potential. On the flip side, they also have the greatest potential for losses. A great aspect of stocks is that they can be very liquid. If you're not relying on your stock returns for a predictable income—if you're not counting on them for funds to cover your daily living expenses—they can be a good way to meet a sudden need. If you have a financial emergency, you could cash them out.

Mutual Funds. One of the good things about mutual funds is that they come already diversified. You don't have to be an expert in the market when you purchase a mutual fund in order to achieve diversification. Mutual funds are also quite often flexible in their initial investment amounts, making them accessible to people from all income levels. Because of this, mutual funds are often considered more secure than stocks and easier for investors to include in their portfolios. Mutual funds have a lower growth potential, but they also have a lower risk for loss. However, here are eleven things you might not know about mutual funds that you should take into consideration:

1. You have no control over your money.

Fund managers will invest in the stocks and the market however they want and according to the mutual fund's objective. You may think that's what you want because you don't understand the ins and outs of the stock market. But don't assume the fund manager understands that much more than you do!

2. There's a huge investment cost.

Every investor in a mutual fund has to bear the cost of investment—in other words, the costs of buying and selling in the market; the taxes applied on the trading; and the costs of marketing, distribution, and managing. Investors pay for all of these. These costs are applied in small percentages, but it takes time for investments to cover them all.

Since your goal is to keep as many dollars as possible, you always want to keep expenses as low as possible and total returns as high as possible. Mutual funds, however, have high expenses, many of which are hidden from view. (We'll talk about this more in the next chapter.)

3. The huge number of choices is confusing.

There are more that forty-five asset management companies, offering more than two thousand mutual funds. It really isn't possible to sort through so many options in order to find something that exactly matches your investment goals. Misleading ads and limited disclosures also create confusion. Open up any financial magazine and you'll see a multitude of advertisements for mutual funds. They all indicate that *their* fund will make you money—but that could very well not be the case.

4. Mutual fund advisors usually add their fees onto what you pay.

We'll talk about this more in the next chapter.

5. The top-performing funds could also be underperformed funds.

This seems counterintuitive, I know, but market performance is seldom constant. Instead, it usually goes in cycles. Because the market is so volatile right now, a fund that was in the top 10 percent of best-performing funds last year could easily be in the lowest 10 percent this year.

6. Index funds have upsides and downsides.

Index funds are mutual funds that are similar to a particular index. When we look at the last twenty years, index funds have given a return that's in the top 10 to 30 percent of all the mutual funds. Index funds can also have drawbacks, however. Investing in index mutual funds can be an excellent low-cost strategy for all or a part of your investment portfolio, but like any other investment strategy, you should work with a financial advisor who can guide you through the ins and outs of index funds. Not all index products are the same, and you need to look beyond the "index fund" label to be sure you are investing in a low-cost product that matches up with your investment strategy.

7. Investments in exchange-traded funds (ETFs) may be better than those in other mutual funds.

ETFs are structured differently from other mutual funds, and they generate fewer capital gains.

8. Mutual funds are excessively diversified.

Diversification is a good thing, right? Mutual funds are a mixture of investments in different companies, industries, and security types, including equities, bonds, and debentures. However the funds are a bit too diversified. Your funds may be distributed so widely that they fail to line up with your actual investment goals.

9. You may pay hidden taxes.

You could be paying taxes on the trading that your fund manager does in buying and selling securities for you.

10. Not all mutual funds allow you to defer taxes.

No mutual fund except for an Equity Linked Savings Scheme (ELSS) allows you to defer taxes.

11. Mutual funds' performance is undermined by the companies that own them.

Many mutual fund companies put generating profits for themselves over accumulating investments for their investors. Mutual fund companies spend a lot of money on advertising and promoting their funds in order to gather assets. Many of the companies also pay brokers incentives to get them to favor their products as a solution for clients. As we've already noted, all of the fees and costs incurred by a mutual fund work against maximizing investors' returns.

Variable Annuities. In past decades, variable annuities had a high potential to make healthy returns on premiums. During the 1980s and 1990s, the stock market saw some of the most significant rises in US history. During that time, the returns on variable annuities could often surpass their fees.

But that's no longer the case. When experts studied hundreds of variable annuities, they found that the total fees can run anywhere from 1.5 to 8 percent per year. A 4 percent total fee level is relatively common with variable annuities that we have reviewed. These fees are charged regardless of whether or not your portfolio actually made any gains.

Here are some of the fees you may pay with a variable annuity:

- administrative expenses
- death benefit fees
- living benefit fees (five types)
- guaranteed lifetime withdrawal benefit fee
- guaranteed minimum accumulation benefit fee

- mortality and expense risk charge

- rider premiums

- underlying fund expenses

- early withdrawal penalty

- premium taxes

- return of principal fee

- turnover ratio fee

Several of these same fees are charged for any annuity, including fixed and indexed annuities. However, *all* of the previous fees are allowable charges for variable annuity products. To get a better understanding, you or your financial advisor can call the company offering the annuity and ask for all the fees that are associated with it. Getting a second opinion or "shopping around" is also a good strategy to ensure that you're getting the most for your money—and not losing it in charges.

MISTAKE 8: TAKING INCOME WITHDRAWALS FROM VEHICLES THAT CAN GO UP AND DOWN

Some investment vehicles might be great assets as pieces of your larger portfolio picture and yet not good for steady, reliable income during retirement. You don't want to have to rely on them for your basic needs. As we discussed in Mistake 1, if you were to withdraw funds while the market was declining, you could easily erode your principal too soon.

As we all know, the market offers no guarantees. If you put yourself into a position where you are relying on income from investment vehicles, you could find yourself withdrawing funds when the market is in a downturn. I can't emphasize this enough: never, ever make withdrawals from a vehicle that is decreasing in value. (We'll also talk about this more in the next chapter.)

If you're relying on these types of investments to cover your necessities, you could be hit twice by a downturn: first, by having to withdraw during market slumps and falling victim to asset erosion, and second, by not having enough time to recover from the market's downturns.

MISTAKE 9: COUNTING ON BONDS FOR INCOME

Bonds are considered to be less risky than many of the other investment vehicles. Unlike those we've talked about so far, bonds are a loan. Unless the issuer defaults, bonds don't rely on the market to do well to produce returns. A bond used to be known for being a conservative asset in your portfolio that could generate stable cash flow, especially during market swings. Even if the issuing company doesn't see gains, the investor is still able to make money from the bond. But can your bond keep pace with inflation? If you purchase a bond that doesn't keep up with the "invisible tax," then you could actually be losing purchasing power of those funds.

Also, keep in mind that not all bonds are the same. In some, the issuer has a right to repay their debt before maturity. Other bonds can be difficult to sell, as many of us learned in 2001 and 2008, when the market experienced a dramatic downturn.

Here are six risks you'll face with bonds:

1. THE RISK OF INTEREST RATES

When interest rates go up, bonds go down. Interest rates will rise eventually, and it could be soon. When they do, your coupon rate (or interest payments) on the bonds you own will not be attractive to buyers. You may have to offer them at a lower price, which enables buyers to get essentially the same return as if they purchased a new bond at the higher rate.

To find out how much exposure your bond has to increasing interest rates, you should understand duration: a number reflecting how much your bond investment will likely change when interest rates rise. For example, let's take a bond fund with a duration of ten years. It will decrease in value by 10 percent if interest rates rise 1 percent; it will decrease by 20 percent if the rise is 2 percent; it will increase by 10 percent if interest rates decline by 1 percent; and so on.

2. THE RISK OF BOND FUNDS

Many people aren't aware that bond funds carry additional risks that individual bonds do not, because they are not sold with a set maturity date in the way that individual ones are. Bond fund returns also decline when interest rates rise.

Fixed-income securities within a bond fund are designed with staggered maturity dates to maintain their purpose as steady income. Bond fund managers replace bonds as they mature, and they may have to sell some holdings to meet their commitments. Sometimes that means selling their higher-yielding bonds, which could be replaced with lower-yield ones. When you discuss bond funds with your financial advisor, you may find they are outside your risk-tolerance comfort zone and that they do not meet your need for reliable income.

3. THE RISK OF CREDIT WORTHINESS

Bond returns depend on the financial stability and projected ability of the bond issuer. Credit rating agencies, such as Moody's and Standard & Poor's, perform this review of corporate or government issuers. Yields to the investor correlate with how much risk is being assumed. High-yield corporate bonds, emerging markets, floating-rate bonds, and low-grade municipals pay the most—but with these bonds you also have a higher risk of the issuer defaulting. Investment-grade corporate bonds are moderate-risk investments, and Treasury bonds are considered the lowest risk.

4. THE RISK OF NOT ENOUGH LIQUIDITY

The bond market is less liquid than the stock market. The ability to sell your bond is dependent on the stock market's ups and downs. Depending on the bond type, you might have to sell for a lower price (or not be able to sell it at all). Government bonds typically sell quickly, while corporate bonds can be more difficult. The smaller the entity issuing the bond, the greater the risk you face.

5. THE RISK OF INFLATION

When inflation is higher, the value of your bond—which is calculated after inflation—can decline. Shorter-term bonds, TIPS (Treasury inflation-protected securities), and commodities like gold are often used to defend bonds against inflation.

6. THE RISK OF REINVESTMENT

When investors' bonds mature while interest rates are decreasing, the bond issuers need to find reinvestment opportunities, which can result in a lower rate of return and less income. Risk levels vary here too by bond type—the higher the coupon, the greater the reinvestment risk.

WE ALL MAKE MISTAKES

If you recognize yourself in any of these common mistakes, don't despair. Ken Poirot wrote, "Wisdom . . . is the result of repeatedly taking corrective action while courageously learning from mistakes."

But it could be that you need to seek out further financial advice. If you started to have doubts about your doctor's ability to guide you to good health, you'd be smart to talk to another health professional about your concerns. The same is true when it comes to your financial health. If your advisor hasn't steered you away from the mistakes I've listed in this chapter, then something is wrong. It could be you need a second opinion.

CHAPTER 4

WHY YOU MIGHT NEED A SECOND OPINION

Back in 1992, my parents were in their early forties. They were both working, and they were in the phase of their lives where they were accumulating savings, putting their money into motion for their retirement. But then my father's accident blew their plans to smithereens. They needed a financial advisor who could help them adjust their investment behaviors to the new situation. They needed to draw income immediately to pay for my father's medical bills, and a good advisor could have helped them do that while still preserving their capital. But that's not what happened.

This was a financially sensitive time in many ways, and they should have been able to trust their advisor to guide them through it. Unfortunately, my parents' broker was not responsive enough to their situation. He didn't give them new advice to meet the needs of their rapidly changing situation. Not only had he not set them up with a backup plan in case something like this happened, he also was unable to help them change course once it did happen. Instead, the only option their advisor gave them was to withdraw money from their investment portfolio. When the stock market is dropping, that's financial suicide.

They ended up doing what's called "reverse dollar cost averaging"—and it destroyed them financially. If only they had gotten a second opinion from another financial advisor, things might have turned out very differently for them.

A DANGEROUS STRATEGY

Let's say you set aside $500 a month to go into your 401(k). That means that in a year, you've contributed $6,000 to your account. A 401(k) isn't like contributing to a savings account, though, where you know exactly how much interest you'll be making on the money you put in. Instead, when the market is up, your monthly $500 buys fewer shares; when the market goes down, that same $500 buys more shares. The plan is that over time, your overall investments will continue to rise. It's called "dollar cost averaging," and it's not a bad strategy when you're in your thirties or forties because you have time to accumulate some money in your investments.

In my parents' case, they suddenly found themselves out of time. They needed income from their investments, so now they were withdrawing money rather than putting it in. This meant that market fluctuations in the market could really hurt them. Dollar cost averaging had turned around.

Here's what happens with reverse dollar cost averaging. Say, for example, you're sixty years old and have $600,000 in your 401(k), when you suddenly find out that because of a health crisis you won't be able to work for at least a year. Your money stays in the same mutual funds where it's always been, and you start taking out regular withdrawals to meet your income needs.

Your original plan was to retire when you had $1 million in your 401(k), at which time you would start making 4 percent withdrawals for income. You were counting on your Social Security payments as well, and you were planning on an annual combined income of about $50,000. Now, however, you're still too young to receive Social Security income, and you have extra medical expenses as well as your normal income needs. You may get some disability insurance, but that doesn't amount to much.

You decide to start making 5 percent withdrawals from your 401(k) to get you through the next year. That will give you a $30,000 annual income. If this happened to be a good year for the stock market, that wouldn't be too much of a problem. As your mutual funds went up, your investments would continue to grow, even though you were taking out income. But what happens if it's a bad year for the market? Let's say your mutual funds dropped in value by 20 percent that year. At the end of the year, your $600,000 would be only $450,000; you lost 20 percent to market losses, and you took out 5 percent. If it turns out you can't go back to work when you thought you could—or you have to retire early and not go back to work at all—that will mean you have to take out money for another year. If you keep your income the same, the percentage of your withdrawal will go up because your account has gone down in value. Now you'll be losing money from your account even faster.

That's reverse dollar averaging. If you keep on doing this, you'll run out of money before you need it most.

As Will Rogers once said, "If you find yourself in a hole, stop digging." You need a new strategy. And if your current financial advisor can't offer you one, then you need a second opinion.

PEACE OF MIND

A new client walked into my office recently and said, "I'm really worried about my retirement funds. The brokerage firm I've been going to says everything is fine. My broker says I have plenty of money and I'll never run out. But I can't shake the feeling that something is wrong. The market goes up and down so much lately. It's gotten so I can't sleep at night because I'm so worried."

This man needed a second opinion. He was in the same situation as the guy who goes to the doctor because he's feeling sick. The doctor checks him over and says to him, "No, I don't see anything wrong with you. You're in good shape. Go home and don't worry." But the guy still feels sick, and he's still worried, so finally he goes to another doctor to get a second opinion. This doctor runs a bunch of tests; she does blood work and sends him for an MRI. Then she runs a few more tests. Each step of the way, she explains to him what she's doing and why. Finally, when all the tests come back, she sits down with him and says, "The bad news is we found a small tumor. But the good news is we caught it in time. It hasn't spread, and you should have a full recovery after treatment."

My new client needed the assurance that someone had checked everything, that any weaknesses in his financial health had been spotted. After he had completed my portfolio stress test, we were able to determine that he did in fact have a problem area in his investments: he was getting dangerously close to reverse dollar cost averaging. Luckily, we were able to take steps to fix the problem by shifting some of his money into more stable investments. I also explained to him why he *didn't* have to worry about some of his other investments that were in pretty good shape. Once I explained everything to him, he felt much better.

The last time I saw him, he said, "Now I can sleep at night again! I finally have some peace of mind. I feel like I have a handle on what's happening."

Another client came in with similar concerns. "I'm really worried about my investments," she told me. "I just can't tell if they're growing the way I need them to. My broker tells me not to worry, but I wish I knew for sure what's going on. I feel so out of control. I have a friend who retired last year, and she found out that she doesn't have anywhere near the income she thought she would. I'm scared that will happen to me."

So, once again, I sat down and started asking questions. "Let me get an idea of your total financial picture," I told her. "Not just your investments in the stock market. Do you have other money or assets somewhere else?"

As I talked to her, I discovered she owned some real estate, which gave her sizable rental income. She also had a large savings account. This time, after I finished my financial stress test with her, I could tell her she was in good shape. She had enough assets that weren't invested in the stock market to more than offset any risk her investment funds were facing. Nevertheless, we eventually decided that she'd be more comfortable moving some of her investment money somewhere less risky.

"I feel so much better now," she told me. "I feel like I'm in control again."

That's what you want from a financial advisor. You want someone who will take the time to go through your portfolio thoroughly, who will let you know if there's anything you should be doing differently, and who will help you understand when you should be worried and when you don't need to be. If you're not getting that from your advisor, go get a second opinion. It's your money. You deserve to know what's going on.

I can pretty much guarantee that you're never going to get that sort of attention from any of the big Wall Street brokers. That's just not the way their businesses are set up. They use slick advertising to convince you to bring their money to them—but once you're there, you're never given the services you need to ensure your retirement plan is safe and stable.

MARKET VOLATILITY

Today's economic markets constantly fluctuate up and down. All that volatility can make you feel a little seasick, especially if you don't understand how it affects your money. There's no telling when another 2008 could happen.

I hear it all the time. "Wait a minute," people say. "When I retired five years ago, the market was booming. I was receiving income just fine because the market was going up and I was taking the gains from my portfolio just the way my advisor had told me to do. But now, every time I turn around the stock market is up three hundred, then it's down three hundred, then it's up again, down again. My advisor tells me to just hold tight, that it will even out in the end and I'll be fine. But how can he be sure? It's not like I have Warren Buffett's net worth! What if the market *really* drops and doesn't go up again for a while? What if I lose my income?"

Once again, this is where a second opinion is essential. Volatility is a fact of life in today's economy. If your portfolio isn't constructed in such a way that it can ride the ups and downs without being damaged, then you could be in big trouble. As you withdraw money from your accounts in retirement, you could see the value on your statements start to decline.

Another new client of mine came to me for that very reason. "My broker keeps saying, 'Sit tight,'" she told me. "But I don't have time to sit tight. I'm in the midst of planning my estate. I can't be sure that when I die the money will be there for the legacy I want to leave."

Another client came in with a similar problem. He was an older man, already in his late seventies, and his wife had Alzheimer's. "I'm sick with worry about our money," he told me. "I don't have time left to ride out whatever it is the market's doing lately. I need to be sure there will be enough money to take care of my wife if something happens to me. Even if I outlive her, I know the day's coming when I won't be able to care for her at home anymore. She's going to need long-term care before too long—and I'm just not sure we'll have enough money to provide that for as long as she needs it."

In both of these cases, I was able to work through my clients' assets and needs in a systematic way. I discovered where they were in good shape and where there were gaps in their projected income. I worked with both clients to make sure all their individual retirement needs were covered.

In order to build a portfolio with lower volatility, your advisor needs to employ a very simple equation:

$$TR = I + G$$

So what the heck does that mean? Well, here's how it works: TR stands for *total return*, which equals *income* (I) added to *growth* (G).

The *income* from your portfolio comes from dividends (in the case of stocks) and interest (in the case of bonds). Unfortunately, you don't get to keep all the income, because sometimes there are expenses, usually in the form of fees.

Growth has to do with both gains and losses. The equation has a plus sign here, but keep in mind that this could actually be a negative number. As we learn in bear markets and downturns like in 2008, sometimes portfolio growth goes down instead of up.

When I'm working with new clients, I usually use this equation in our second meeting in order to get a good picture of how their investments are structured. The best way to compensate for market volatility is to depend more on income than you do on growth. Otherwise, if you're counting on growth more than income, you'll see some wild swings in your total numbers. Those flip-flops can make you feel pretty anxious when you're trying to get to sleep at night!

DO YOU HAVE A RELATIONSHIP WITH YOUR BROKER?

So many of my new clients come in with these kinds of concerns. They may have a statement from their broker that lists their stocks and bonds, their mutual funds, a life insurance policy, and maybe an annuity. It's a standard package I've seen a hundred times before. So I sit down with them and ask them some questions.

"Do you have an exit strategy?"

They usually look at me kind of blankly and say, "What's that?"

"Well, say a catastrophe happens that changes your life significantly. What if you had to start drawing on your retirement funds earlier than expected? What's your backup plan?"

"I'm only in my forties," they might say (or they might say their thirties or even their fifties). "I'm not going to retire for a long time."

They see themselves as being in the middle of the accumulation phase of their lives. They're earning money, setting aside money for a retirement that still seems like a long time from now.

So I list some situations that might disrupt their plans, crises that could bring their accumulation phase to a sudden end. "Do you know where you'd be able to draw money from without disrupting your plan for ongoing income?" I ask. Now they're starting to look a little worried. "Do you know what would be the most tax-efficient way to get money to get you through a crisis?"

They usually look uncomfortable and shrug their shoulders. I know they don't have a clue what the answers are to my questions, but they say, "Well, I'm sure my broker knows the answers to those questions. I just leave everything up to him."

"When was the last time you talked to him?" I ask.

"Uh, last year, I think," they might say. Nine times out of ten, they haven't talked to their broker for at least six months.

"And has anything changed in your life over the past year?"

"Not really," they usually say. But then when I ask them a few questions, I find out that actually things *have* changed quite a bit. They have an adult child who's moved back in with them; they've taken on the expense of sending a grandchild to college; they had to dip into their savings to buy a new car sooner than they had expected to; or maybe they have some new goals for the future that they didn't before.

"Tell me," I say to them, "do you feel as though you have a relationship with your broker? Does he know who you are personally? Has he taken the time to really get to know you?"

By this time, they're really looking uneasy. "He's a busy guy," they mutter. "I just want him to take care of my money. I don't expect him to be my best friend."

Well, no. Your financial advisor *shouldn't* be your best friend. But getting to know their clients is part of all good advisors' job. They should never be too busy to sit down and talk with you. Your money isn't just money. It's your life; it's what you're counting on for all the everyday expenses of living, as well as all the unexpected ones. So you need—and you deserve—someone who understands what you need, who truly sees your best interests as part of their job.

YOUR BEST INTERESTS

Recently the medical world has come under scrutiny. Surveys conducted in 2004 and again in 2009 showed that more than three-quarters of doctors had at least one type of financial relationship with a drug or medical device company.[19] In 2013, pharmaceu-

19 Eric G. Campbell et al., "Physician Professionalism and Changes in Physician-Industry Relationships From 2004 to 2009," *Archives of Internal Medicine*, 2010;170(20):1820-1826. DOI:10.1001/

tical companies paid out a total of $1.4 billion to doctors. These companies also do little things like take doctors out to lunch and give them gifts. Researchers say that all this can influence a doctor's perception of a drug and lead to more prescribing of it.[20] I don't know about you, but I don't want my doctor prescribing a medicine to me based on his relationship with the company that manufactures it; I want to be certain that any drug he prescribes to me is based on his evaluation of my individual needs.

There's something similar going on in the financial advisory world that's equally concerning. The 401(k) industry calls it revenue sharing; the mutual fund industry refers to it as subtransfer agency fees, shareholder servicing fees, and profit-sharing payments; and the US Department of Labor calls it indirect payments. These fees are paid by mutual funds to 401(k) providers who perform the record-keeping function for the plans. Where does the money come from for these fees? It's charged against the mutual funds, reducing investment returns. That's a problem when these fees are hidden and folks don't know where their money is actually going. But what's even more concerning is that financial advisors, like physicians, are bound to be influenced by companies that are paying them money.

It's not only fees that connect financial advisors and mutual funds. The large brokerage firms charge fund families for access to their customers. At Morgan Stanley, for example, a fund family has to pay the firm at least $250,000 and up to 0.16 percent of clients' investment in its funds. For $350,000 to $750,000, fund families can also make special presentations to Morgan Stanley brokers and

archinternmed.2010.383.

20 Charles Ornstein and Eric Sagara, "How Much Are Drug Companies Paying Your Doctor?" *Scientific American*, September 30, 2014, http://www.scientificamerican.com/article/how-much-are-drug-companies-paying-your-doctor.

be speakers at its conferences.[21] All the big Wall Street brokers do the same sort of thing. So when you get financial advice from one of these guys, how can you be sure that he has your best interests in mind? Well, you can't.

Brokers also get paid based on their quotas and commissions. It's to their advantage to have as many clients as possible, so it's hard for them to spend much time with each person. They want to get people in and get them out. They also get other kickbacks from certain investment funds—so of course they're motivated to sell those to their clients, regardless of whether they're the best options for their clients' actual needs. This is causing a dangerous disconnect between investors and their financial representatives.

Starting back in 2015, the Obama administration expressed its concern about the situation and got the ball rolling toward a monumental change in the financial industry. *The Wall Street Journal* reported that President Barack Obama endorsed stricter standards for brokers and others who recommend retirement-account investments, backing new rules requiring advisors to put their clients' interests ahead of personal gain.

The Labor Department rules that are to go into effect April 2017 are expected to chip away at lucrative sources of income for brokers by making them adhere to loftier standards of "fiduciary" service. Wall Street groups have been fighting moves to ratchet up industry standards, maintaining they already operate under strict rules and warning that the new standards could remove an incentive for brokers to serve accounts with smaller balances.

21 Leslie P. Norton, "When Fund Companies Pay to Play, So Do You," *Barrons*, April 12, 2014, http://www.barrons.com/articles/SB50001424053111904223604579487610336424326.

These so-called fiduciary standards for financial advisors would help to address an area of widespread confusion about how financial professionals are paid. Currently, brokers' recommendations for 401(k) plans and other retirement accounts generally must be "suitable" for an investor. But they are not required to be in an investor's best interests, a standard known as fiduciary. This results in a weaker standard that critics say permits high fees that eat into investors' returns.[22]

For decades, brokers and other financial advisors have operated on a commission model in which they get paid a fee when customers buy or sell securities. The new rules would apply a fiduciary standard that currently applies to advisors who merely sell financial products (such as advising to open a rollover IRA account). The rule is intended to protect Americans from advisors who are pushing stocks and mutual funds that may not be best for the customers.[23]

As you can probably imagine, the Wall Street brokerage firms are fighting the changes. They continue to appeal and insist that the rules limit the range of retirement products that brokers can pitch or make advice too costly for many investors. In other words, their brokers would no longer be able to offer their clients retirement products that weren't truly in their clients' best interests! They argue that maintaining a "fiduciary standard" would cost more because advisors would need to spend more time talking with clients to ascertain the best advice to give them.[24] To cover their costs, the advisors would likely

---

22 Andrew Ackerman and Karen Damato, "Obama Backs New Rules for Brokers on Retirement Accounts," *The Wall Street Journal*, February 23, 2015, http://www.wsj.com/articles/obama-to-back-new-rules-for-brokers-on-retirement-accounts-1424689201.

23 "Obama Targets Financial Advisors," *Wall Street Journal*, August 16, 2015, http://www.wsj.com/articles/obama-targets-financial-advisers-1439763731.

24 Ibid.

adjust their practices to focus on the bigger fish or clients with more money to afford the increased fees.

Is that what you want from your financial advisor—someone who is charging you hidden fees to pay for their time, who needs to get you in and out of her office so that she can maintain her quota of clients?

Whenever I talk to prospective clients about their current portfolios, I always ask, "How did you come up with this portfolio? What do you know about these mutual funds?" Nine times out of ten, people say that their broker picked the funds—and the people themselves really know nothing about them.

Reading mutual fund prospectuses is confusing, I know, but if you go through all fifty to one hundred pages (or more), you'll find the true operating expense charges and fees. Most people don't take the time to read the prospectus, though. That's one reason they hired an advisor in the first place.

When I see someone come into my office with a portfolio from one of the big brokerage firms, I don't even have to look inside to know what I'll find. I know that Firm A consistently uses XYZ mutual fund, and Firm B consistently uses ABC mutual fund. So sometimes when people say, "I'm with Firm A," I say, "Before I open up your statement, tell me—do you have XYZ mutual fund in your portfolio?"

They always look surprised. They say something like, "Well, yeah, actually, we do. How'd you know? That's a great company, right?"

"What do you actually know about the company?" I ask.

"Well," they say, "my broker picked it for me."

"But you know nothing about it? Do you know why it's part of your portfolio?"

"What do you mean?" they ask me.

"What's the philosophy behind having this particular fund in your portfolio?"

"Well, it's a growth portfolio."

And that's pretty much all they know.

When the next person walks into my office with a portfolio from Firm B, I can do the same thing. When I see ten different people with Firm B that have pretty much the same portfolio, I get concerned. I know these folks' brokers can't possibly be giving their clients the attention they need. They're not taking the time to match up each client individually with the best possible plan.

I suspect sometimes it really is a question of time as much as kickbacks and revenue sharing. People get lazy. Brokers get in the habit of using the same formula over and over. The funds they pick may be based more on their own personal philosophy—and then they just keep picking them over and over. They've put together a portfolio including ABC or XYZ so many times that they don't even notice that some of the funds they're using have overlapping stocks. How can you call that diversification?

This is the sort of thing that shows up when I give people the financial stress test. My clients are always shocked. They may have worked with their brokers for the past twenty years or so, and they've totally trusted them. "Why would he do that to me?" they ask. "We've been friends for years!"

These brokers may be perfectly nice people. They're not intending to hurt their clients, any more than a doctor would intentionally prescribe the wrong medicine. But people are only human. They get used to doing things a certain way. They have blind spots when it comes to their own behaviors. They get defensive when people criticize them. And they're resistant to change. Like I said, it's only human.

But that's why it's always a good idea to get a second opinion. A professional who looks at things differently, who's able to work outside the box and think creatively on your behalf, may be able to cast fresh light on your situation.

That's what a woman named Mary was looking for when she came into my office recently. She wanted me to take a look at her portfolio and her retirement plan, just so she could get a second opinion. She was planning to retire in about six months, and she wanted to be sure everything was in good shape. So I ran the stress test on her portfolio. I looked at all the numbers. And I found something that concerned me.

Mary had an annuity. She was planning on getting $27,000 of yearly income from it once she retired. Her advisor had told her there was a 1.2 percent fee on it, but she wasn't exactly sure what that would mean for her.

"Let's call the insurance company and find out," I said.

We got a representative from the insurance company on the line. Using the speakerphone, I asked her to pull up Mary's contract and walk through it with us. Then I asked some very basic questions. I got a list of all the fees on the account. Once we were off the phone, I added up everything and did the math.

It turned out Mary was actually paying 3.1 percent in fees, and there were also a few other expenses she hadn't been aware of. In the end, the fees added up to about $28,000 a year. She was paying more in fees each year than she was planning to take in income! Inevitably, she was going to run out of money.

Mary still had time to make some changes. We worked together to create a new plan that would truly work to her benefit. I brought in my company's team of specialists to sit down with her to determine the best annuity to meet her needs. In the end, we brought four or five options to the table, and then we went through each of them, listing the pros and cons. Some were better for her short-term income needs; some had better death benefits. We talked over all of them with Mary and listened to what she had to say. When we were done, all of us—including Mary—felt confident that her retirement plan was in good shape. She would have the income she needed during retirement. I'm so glad she got a second opinion because it made all the difference in her future security.

Did Mary's broker intentionally set things up so that Mary would face financial disaster? I'm sure he didn't. He just didn't take the time to look at everything carefully. He didn't take her situation seriously enough to give it his full attention.

I have to say, the new Department of Labor rules for a fiduciary standard among brokerage firms will go a long way toward cleaning up the negative perception that many people have about investment brokers. Anyone who helps you and advises you with something as crucial as your nest egg for retirement *should* have your best interests in mind all of the time. If you get any sense that your advisors have other interests in mind, ask them about their fiduciary standards.

NOT ALL FINANCIAL ADVISORS
ARE THE SAME

Most people, when they seek medical advice, have no problem understanding the concept of specialization. You don't go to an orthodontist for a heart problem. You don't ask your podiatrist to do brain surgery. But when it comes to financial planning, the impression a lot of folks have is that all financial advisors are cut from the same bolt of cloth. Nothing could be further from the truth.

A few years ago, when I got up to give a talk to a roomful of union workers, an interesting thing happened. Before I could continue with my speech, I was interrupted with a few boos and some snickers. One gentleman went so far as to say that people in my profession were the cause of all of his financial woes.

Needless to say, this reaction upset me greatly. It also was an awakening of sorts. If that was his opinion about financial advisors, then perhaps many others had the same perception. The outspoken gentleman, I learned later, had a sizable portion of his portfolio invested in the stock market when it crashed in 2008. He and millions of others saw chunks of their life savings disappear overnight. Some of these individuals were young enough to earn and save their dollars back. Some were so wealthy they didn't even feel the pinch. But by far the vast majority of the people who were hurt by that financial disaster were those who were ill prepared to lose such a significant portion of their savings. Of course, few of these individuals managed their own money. Most of them had it parked with companies whose officers' business cards read . . . yep, you guessed it: one of those big-name brokerage firms!

No wonder this gentleman reacted the way he did. From his perspective, I was one of those people who lost him all that money in 2008! He had the mistaken impression that all financial advisors are risk-oriented financial advisors, the kind that focus more on the return on the money than the return of the money. From his point of view, and I suspect that of many others, all financial advisors are alike.

I couldn't blame him for his misconception. When people in my profession sit down with new clients, many of them don't make a distinction as to whether they work on the risk side or on the safety side of financial coaching. The media certainly hasn't done a thorough job of making the distinction between risk-oriented financial advisors and safe-money financial advisors. That's why my firm adheres to a strict low volatility investment discipline. We provide plans that will allow you to thrive in retirement with more modest returns and less risk of large losses.

ACCUMULATION PLANNERS AND RETIREMENT PLANNERS

There is a big difference between what I like to call "accumulation planners" and retirement planners.

Accumulation planners are in the majority. They evolved during the bull run of the 1980s and 1990s. Decades later, if you're still in the pre-retirement stage of life, odds are good this is the type of advisor you are still working with today. During the accumulation phase of your life, you are working and earning, and hopefully saving and investing. These advisors help you with your investments. That's okay because when you're younger, some investment risk is appropriate. You have time on your side. The objective is for your money to steadily replicate itself as you add to it.

One day, though, when the time is right, you plan to collect your last paycheck, wave goodbye to the workday, and allow that nest egg to fund your retirement. Appropriately, you invested for growth, using stocks, bonds, mutual funds, real estate investment trusts, options, maybe even variable annuities. You assumed the risk that accompanied these investment choices. The job of your advisor was to grow your assets at risk levels appropriate to your age and your risk tolerance, until one day, you ease off the risk pedal, put the brakes on, and make a major change in direction.

At this point, you tell your broker, who may very well have done a great job getting you to where you are today, that you appreciate the service and now you are no longer willing or able to assume as much risk as you previously did. You are now in a position where you must depend on your savings for daily expenses. You will be writing your own paycheck, so to speak, from your retirement nest egg. This means these assets must be preserved and carefully distributed, not placed at undue risk for the purposes of growth. Let's say you're savvy enough to know that you need to explain to your accumulation advisor that you are now in need of three things: safety, preservation of assets, and dependable income.

Your advisor says, "Sure, we can do that! Let's restructure." He then proceeds to reallocate your assets, putting you into bond funds, variable annuities, and fixed income investments. All seems to be going well.

But wait a minute. You want to hear your advisor use words like "guarantee" and "safe," but instead you are hearing words like "projection" and "probable." In other words, your assets are still at risk. So what do you do now? To be perfectly candid, it's time to find a different advisor—one who specializes in retirement income planning, one whose focus is on working with individuals who are at or near retirement.

PAULA AND THE SALESMAN

To understand what's going on here a bit better, think about the process of shopping for a new car. Let's say the person who needs the new car is Paula, a young, unmarried woman just starting her career. She doesn't have a huge income, but she needs a car to drive back and forth to work. Her priorities are:

- **affordability:** low monthly payments

- **gas mileage:** thirty-five miles per gallon or more

- **compact:** needs to fit in a small garage

Paula walks into a car dealership and meets Ben, the car salesman. She explains what she's looking for, and Ben says, "I am highly trained and very experienced, and I know exactly what you need."

Paula thinks to herself, *This salesman seems to be sensitive to my needs and knows exactly what he is talking about. Good!*

Ben then proceeds to show her a big, black Hummer H1, the biggest, baddest Hummer money can buy. Paula, who is now starting to question the salesman's judgment, says, "It's beautiful, but I have a small garage and it certainly won't fit."

Ben says, "Not a problem. I have a great relationship with a contractor who focuses solely on garages."

Paula, starting to suspect that maybe the salesman just isn't catching on, tells him that fifteen miles per gallon isn't exactly fuel efficient, and she can't afford the cost of the Hummer H1, let alone the cost of constructing a new garage in which to park it.

Ben, still scrambling for a solution, says, "Now I know what you need." He takes Paula over to the smaller Hummer H3.

Paula is getting frustrated. She wonders why this salesman isn't listening. Why is he trying to sell her a four-wheel-drive monster with a $40,000 price tag, which is still way outside her price range?

But Ben tells her not to worry. "Paula, we are running a special this month," he tells her. "Your monthly payments will be only $525."

"But I can't afford that!" Paula says. Discouraged and puzzled, she heads for the door. As she walks away, she happens to look back and see the sign. The words "Hummer Dealership" are spelled out clearly in large block letters that measure at least two feet tall. Now she understands why Ben offered her a Hummer. Hummers were all he had to sell.

Seeking advice from financial advisors whose scope is limited to the accumulation side of the financial world is likely to produce similar results. They really only have one kind of product to sell. And unfortunately, in the financial advisory world, the signs usually aren't as easy to spot.

The story about Paula and the Hummer dealer may be a bit outlandish, but it's not all that different in substance from some I've heard from retirees and pre-retirees when they describe their experiences with the financial advisors with whom they worked. When these folks reached that zone where they needed safety and income, their current advisors only knew accumulation and continued to offer risk investments with all the bells and whistles. It's not the advisors' fault. They were doing everything they know how to do—but risk investment was all they knew.

HOW TO RECOGNIZE THE DIFFERENCES BETWEEN ACCUMULATION AND RETIREMENT SPECIALISTS

Looking for the right financial advice can be hard if you don't know what to look for. Look at it this way. You are, in effect, interviewing candidates to determine whom you will select to be your personal "retirement doctor." As with any interview process, you'll be able to make a more intelligent choice if you listen carefully to what comes out of the interviewee's mouth. If you are dealing with an accumulation specialist, you'll hear certain words and expressions. You will likely be told these three things in the following order:

- **Return:** You may hear advisors say, "This investment should return 7 percent a year." Or, "This mutual fund has returned 6 percent per year over the last ten years." There is a strong focus on year-over-year returns rather than income. Return is the price appreciation as opposed to income, which is the amount generated in interest or dividend.

- **Safety:** After you hear about the return, your natural reaction is to ask how safe that investment is. You may hear advisors discuss the assets, the balance sheet, their diversification across sectors, the experience of the investment team, or how long they have been in the business. But you won't hear them explain how safe your investment actually is.

- **Income:** Last, you will hear about the income, yield, or dividends that are produced. You may hear expressions like "It has 5 percent yield" or "This mutual fund has created 4 percent per year in income."

Please note that income is usually the last thing discussed in this dialogue, when, in retirement situations, it should be the first thing on the list.

On the other hand, when you listen to a retirement specialist, you will hear about these three things in the following order:

- **Income:** You will hear about guaranteed retirement income, yield, or dividends. The most important thing in retirement is guaranteed income, so shouldn't that be what is discussed first when it comes to your investments?

- **Safety:** You will hear about the Legal Reserve System, the guarantees provided, and how those guarantees are backed.

- **Return:** Last, return is discussed: the return on your investments, not the assets you require to support your lifestyle. My father is fond of this expression: "It's not the return on your money that is critical in retirement; it is the return of your money."

Listen for these expressions and use them as a gauge to determine whether your advisor, or potential advisor, is on the accumulation side or the retirement side of advising. Once you determine which type of advisor is sitting on the other side of the table, you can easily determine if a second meeting is worthwhile. Keep in mind that your retirement advisor's job is not to make you rich but to do everything in his power to make sure you will never be poor.

MAKE SURE YOU HAVE THE GUIDE YOU NEED

As I've just explained, the advisor who helped you accumulate money may not be the right person to help you when you enter the phase of your life where you need to take out your money for income. You need different financial strategies now from what you did during the growth phase of your life. Not getting a second opinion could be fatal.

This always makes me think of the story about the first men to climb Mount Everest. Sir Edmund Hillary gets the credit for leading the first successful expedition to the top of Mount Everest in 1952. The Queen of England awarded him the knighthood for his achievement. In fact, though, Hillary wasn't the first person to reach Mount Everest's summit. Twenty-eight years earlier, George Mallory got there. So why does Hillary always get the credit for being the first? Because Hillary didn't just make it to the peak; he also successfully led his expedition back down the mountain. George Mallory didn't. He died on the mountainside.

Edmund Hillary probably wasn't any smarter or stronger than Mallory was, but he did do something different: he didn't use the same Sherpa to guide his expedition down the mountain as he'd used going up. Sherpas, as you probably know, are the people of the Khumbu Valley, the area surrounding Everest. Living at high altitudes for generations, they have developed a genetic natural strength for mountain climbing. They are Mount Everest experts. People who want to climb Mount Everest know they need a Sherpa they can trust who will show them the way. But not all Sherpas have the same skills. They don't all know the same paths, and they don't use the same strategies. So you need a Sherpa with one set of skills to get you up Mount Everest, and you need another one to get you down.

It's pretty much the same with financial advisors. The advisor who helped you accumulate money may not be the right advisor to help you during retirement. You've climbed the financial mountain— but now you want to be sure you can go down the other side.

I hear people say, "My financial advisor is great. Over the past twenty years, he's helped me make a ton of money. I trust him absolutely."

These folks' advisors may very well deserve their clients' trust. But if their advisors' skills are focused on picking investments for growth—for accumulation—they may not know the strategies their clients need during retirement, where the priority now is to preserve their income for the rest of their lives.

Oscar Wilde said, "When I was young, I thought that money was the most important thing. Now that I'm old, I *know* that it is." When you're in the working phase of your life, earning and saving money may seem like a priority. But it's when you reach retirement that you really realize how much your well-being depends on having the money you need.

You've worked hard all your life. When it's time for your retirement, you deserve to relax a little. You don't need the anxiety of trying to keep pace with the ever-so-volatile stock market. You need someone who can guide you safely through these years, someone who can make a structured plan that will give you both the income and the peace of mind you need. Make certain your financial advisor can give you that. Get a second opinion so you can be sure.

And then keep in mind that if you're thinking about retirement, you should also be thinking about planning your estate (if you haven't already). You may need still another specialist to help you with this part of your long-term financial health.

CHAPTER 5

ESTATE PLANNING ESSENTIALS

John P. DeSantis

I will begin with the age old question: **Have you done your estate planning?** As an estate planning attorney with over twenty years experience meeting with clients and presenting seminars on this topic, I can tell you that although most people think they have effectively done their estate planning, the sad reality is that they have not. I believe the reason for this is that most people misunderstand what estate planning means and how it is effectuated.

WHAT IS ESTATE PLANNING?

Estate planning is the process we engage in during our lives the objectives of which are usually to accomplish the following: (1) ensuring that our assets pass to the appropriate parties, (2) minimization of any estate and inheritance taxes, and (3) naming people to make our medical and financial decisions in the event we become incompetent.

HOW DO YOU EFFECTUATE YOUR ESTATE PLAN?

You effectuate your estate plan by (1) executing the **appropriate documents** and (2) **titling your assets** correctly.

APPROPRIATE DOCUMENTS

At a minimum, everyone should consider executing a health-care directive (living will), power of attorney, and will.

1. **Health-Care Directive (Living Will).** A health-care directive is a document that gives an individual ("medical agent") the authority to make medical decisions for you in the event you become incapacitated. In the event that your medical agent needs to act on your behalf, it is imperative that he or she be fully apprised of your medical condition; and as such, it is essential that your health-care directive grant your medical agent the authority to access your medical records as well as the ability to communicate with your health-care providers. If your health-care directive does not grant your medical agent these powers, your health-

care providers may not share your medical information with your agent for fear of violating the Health Insurance Portability and Accountability Act (HIPPA). Lastly, it is important that you appoint successor medical agents in the event that the initially named medical agent is unavailable or unable to make your medical decisions.

2. **Power of Attorney.** A power of attorney is a document that authorizes an individual ("financial agent") to make financial decisions for you in the event you become incapacitated. Your power of attorney should specifically authorize your financial agent to, among other things: (1) dispose of, exchange, or encumber your real estate; (2) apply for, obtain, and maintain governmental benefits (i.e. Social Security, Medicare, Medicaid, etc.); (3) exercise all rights, powers, elections, waivers, and authorities over your retirement plans and digital assets (i.e. desktops, laptops, smartphones, etc.); and (4) gift your cash or property to your family and trusts for the benefit of your family. The gifting provision in your power of attorney is essential, as it allows your financial agent to engage in Medicaid and/or estate planning in the event of your incapacitation.

    Although your power of attorney can become effective (i.e. your financial agent can act on your behalf) either upon (1) your incapacity (i.e. springing power of attorney) or (2) the date you execute your power of attorney (i.e. immediate power of attorney), it is my recommendation that you have it effective the date you execute it. If your power of attorney is effective upon your incapacity, then your financial agent will have to prove that you are incapacitated each time he or she acts on your behalf. Usually, in order to prove incapacitation, institutions will want two (2) recently dated letters from doctors stating that you are incapacitated. Doctors may be reluctant to provide your financial agent with such a letter for legal and medical reasons (i.e. the person who executed the power of attorney is in the early stages of dementia and sometimes has capacity and sometimes not). Finally, it is important to appoint successor financial agents in the event that your initially named financial agent is unavailable or unable to make your financial decisions.

3. **Will.** A will is a document that, upon your demise, grants an individual (i.e. an executor/executrix) the power to (1) gather your probate assets, (2) pay your debts, and (3) distribute your remaining probate assets (i.e. the assets remaining after the payment of any debts) to the people/entities named in your will. If you have a minor child, it is also vital to name a guardian for the child and direct the assets bequeathed to the child be placed in trust for the child until such time as you feel he or she would be mature enough to handle those assets. Notice I used the words "probate assets."

WHAT ARE PROBATE ASSETS?

Probate assets are the assets that (1) are held in the decedent's name alone (i.e. not joint) and (2) have no beneficiary designation. Why is this important? Let's look at the following example.

Global Example 1. Fred's will provides that all of his assets will go to his wife, Wilma. Fred dies (1) survived by Wilma and his child, Pebbles, and (2) owning the following assets:

House (joint with Wilma)	$500,000
IRA (beneficiary, Pebbles)	$100,000
Securities	$300,000
Cash (joint with Pebbles)	$100,000

Question: Which of Fred's assets will pass by virtue of his will to Wilma?

(A) All of them
(B) Only the house and cash
(C) Only the IRA
(D) Only the securities

The answer is D. Did you get it right? Why just the securities? The securities are the only assets that are in Fred's name alone and which have no beneficiary designation. **That is right, only your probate assets will pass under your will.** This leads me to the next topic

ASSET TITLING

That's right . . . asset titling. Asset titling is as important as executing the "appropriate documents." Remember, in order to effectuate your estate plan, you need to execute the "appropriate documents" and correctly title your assets ("asset titling").

Probate assets—Assets that pass by will

As *Global Example 1* illustrates, only your probate assets (assets in your name alone that have no beneficiary designation) would pass under your will.

Jointly held assets—Assets that pass by operation of law

Assets held jointly with another person pass at your death by **"operation of law"** to the surviving joint person and therefore do not pass pursuant to the terms of your will. Most states have a law that stipulates, at your death, any asset owned jointly with another person will pass by operation of law to such person. That is why, in *Global Example 1*, Fred's house and cash do not pass under his will but rather by operation of law to the surviving joint person, namely, Wilma and Pebbles, respectively. Example of assets passing by "operation of law" include assets titled as follows: John and Mary JWROS (Joint with Rights of Survivorship), John and Mary joint tenants, and if married, John and Mary, husband and wife or John and Mary, tenants by the entirety.

Assets with a beneficiary designation— Assets that pass by contract

Assets that have a designated beneficiary will pass at death to such named beneficiary (i.e. by contract), and accordingly, will not pass pursuant to the terms of your will. Whenever you execute a beneficiary form (i.e. contract), you are directing the institution holding your asset to pay that asset to the beneficiary named on such form. That is why, in *Global Example 1*, Fred's IRA does not pass under his will but by contract to the named beneficiary, Pebbles. Examples of assets that can pass by contract include, but are not limited to: IRAs, 401(k)s, 403(b)s, 457 plans, annuities, payable on death ("POD") accounts, transfer on death ("TOD") accounts, profit-sharing plans, deferred compensation plans, and life insurance.

As you now know, only those assets that are in your name alone and that have no beneficiary designation will pass by the terms of your will. For those of you who like mnemonics, COW is how assets pass at your demise.

C = CONTRACT

O = OPERATION OF LAW

W = WILL

What percentage of your estate will pass by virtue of your will? The following equation will help you to determine same:

Entire estate:	100%
Less: Percentage of estate passing by:	
(1)Contract	(---%)
(2)Operation of law	(---%)
Equals: Percentage of estate passing by will	----%

If you are married, it would not be surprising if you told me that less than 20 percent of your assets would pass by virtue of your will when you die. Does that bother you? It should; isn't one of the main reasons you execute a will is to direct who gets your assets and how at your demise? Or maybe it doesn't bother you because you are thinking (1) my will states that my spouse gets my assets, (2) my assets that pass by contract all name my spouse as the primary beneficiary, and (3) my assets that pass by operation of law are all jointly owned with my spouse. So no matter how my assets pass at my death (i.e. "COW"), my spouse would get them. Well, let's see if asset titling really does matter. Up to this point, we have not discussed what our politicians are always arguing about—you guessed it—estate taxes!

ESTATE TAXES

Just like you may have to pay federal and state income taxes each calendar year, when you die, depending upon the size of your estate and who you bequeath it to, you (well, actually your estate) may also have to pay federal and state estate taxes. Thankfully, in most jurisdictions, there is no limit on the amount of property that you can bequeath to your US citizen spouse. In tax jargon, this unlimited amount that you can bequeath to your US citizen spouse is referred to as the **unlimited marital deduction**. If you leave property to anyone other than your US citizen spouse, then if your taxable estate exceeds the following thresholds, estate taxes will have to be paid.

	TAX-FREE THRESHOLD	TAX RATE(S) IF EXCEED THRESHOLD
Federal Estate Tax	$5,450,000 (2016) *	40%
New Jersey Estate Tax	$675,000 (2016) **/***	Up to 16% (sliding scale)

*Indexed for inflation so this threshold amount may increase each calendar year.

**New Jersey's Estate Tax Exemption will be (1) increased to $2,000,000 for calendar year 2017 and (2) eliminated in its entirety effective January 1, 2018.

***New Jersey also has an inheritance tax (bequests to spouses, children, grandchildren, and parents will not trigger this tax) and your estate will pay the greater of the estate tax, if any, or the inheritance tax.

If a single person in New Jersey can leave $675,000 to his or her children without the imposition of New Jersey estate tax, how much do you think a married couple living in New Jersey can leave their children, New Jersey estate tax free? Did you guess $1,350,000 ($675,000 multiplied by two people)? Let's see if you are correct.

Although the following example assumes that the 2016 New Jersey estate tax exemption will apply, it is critical to understand that the concepts set forth in the example; namely, (1) titling your assets correctly ("asset titling") and (2) executing the appropriate documents will remain important even after the New Jersey estate tax exemption is increased and then repealed.

Global Example 2. Tony and Carmela (both US citizens) are married, live in New Jersey, and have two adult children. Tony and Carmela each own the following assets:

ASSET	TONY	CARMELA
House	$675,000	
Cash		$675,000

Tony dies and his will bequeaths his entire estate to Carmela. Since Tony owned the house in his name alone, it would pass by the terms of his will to Carmela. Now Carmela owns the house and the cash, which assets total $1,350,000. Carmela now dies bequeathing her entire estate to her and Tony's two children. As Carmela's estate exceeds $675,000 (the New Jersey threshold), the children would have to pay New Jersey estate taxes totaling approximately $54,800. What happened? Didn't we just conclude that a married couple living in New Jersey could leave $1,350,000 to their children New Jersey estate tax free? What went wrong?

Answer: Tony and Carmela executed "simple" or "I love you" wills. Tony left his entire estate to Carmela, leaving Carmela with $1,350,000, and as such, Tony forfeited his right to give $675,000 to the children New Jersey estate tax free. Should Tony have given his entire estate ($675,000) to the children and not his wife, Carmela? I bet you Carmela would not be too happy with that suggestion. So, in the above example, how could Tony and Carmela have left their children $1,350,000 estate tax free in New Jersey without disinheriting each other? The answer is they would have needed to execute "tax-sensitive" wills (i.e. "Appropriate Documents").

Tax-Sensitive Wills

Instead of executing "simple" wills in the above example, Tony and Carmela should have executed "tax-sensitive" wills. If they had done so, both Tony and Carmela's wills would have contained the following provisions:

1. If my spouse survives me, my executor shall distribute, from my residuary estate, to the trustee of my bypass trust, an amount equal to the largest amount that will not result in any state (i.e. New Jersey) estate tax payable.

2. If my spouse survives me, my executor shall distribute the remaining balance of my residuary estate to my spouse outright.

Assuming Tony and Carmela did not make any taxable gifts during their lifetimes, now, upon Tony's demise, instead of the house worth $675,000 (the largest amount that will not result in any New Jersey estate tax) going to Carmela outright, it would have gone into the bypass trust (also known as a credit shelter trust) for the benefit of Carmela. As Tony did not have any assets exceeding $675,000, Carmela would not have received any assets outright from Tony. As such, after Tony's demise, the house (worth $675,000) would be owned by the bypass trust (for the benefit of Carmela) and the cash ($675,000) would be owned by Carmela. **Now upon Carmela's subsequent demise, there would be no New Jersey estate tax due, as Carmela's estate would only include the cash ($675,000) and not the house, which is owned by the bypass trust. By executing "tax-sensitive" wills, Tony and Carmela saved their children $54,800 in New Jersey estate tax.**

But, if you were Carmela, you would probably say to the advisor, "So the kids save $54,800 after Tony and I are dead, but what about me? If Tony and I executed "simple" wills and Tony died, I would own assets worth $1,350,000 (house plus cash) and the kids, after my death, would then owe $54,800. Yes, executing "tax-sensitive" wills saves the kids money but what access do I have over the assets owned by the bypass trust?" The advisor's response would be, "Carmela that is an excellent question." The advisor would then tell Carmela the following about Tony's bypass trust.

Tony's Bypass Trust (Credit Shelter Trust)

"Carmela, you would be (1) the trustee (i.e. manager) of the bypass trust, (2) able to spend the income and principal of the bypass trust for your living expenses (i.e. your health, maintenance, and support), and (3) able to gift the assets in the bypass trust to your descendants. Even though you would be given all of these rights over the assets in the bypass trust, the bypass trust would not be includable in your estate when you die." **Yes, I will repeat what the advisor just told**

Carmela: the bypass trust would not be includable in Carmela's estate upon her demise.

Now that Tony and Carmela are satisfied that the surviving spouse would have total access to their own assets and the assets in the bypass trust, they can have their attorney prepare "tax-sensitive" wills ("appropriate documents") for both of them. However, what if, in the example, Tony and Carmela executed the "tax-sensitive" wills but their attorney never obtained a listing of their assets which now consists of the following:

OWNERSHIP OF ASSET

ASSET	JOINT	TONY	CARMELA
Brokerage Account (Stocks and Bonds)	$400,000		
Bank Accounts (Payable on Death to Spouse)		$200,000	$75,000
Securities (Individually Owned)		$275,000	
House			$400,000

Upon Tony's demise, which asset(s) do you think would have gone into his bypass trust for the benefit of Carmela? **Before answering, I hope you remember that "asset titling" (i.e. "COW") is as important as executing the "appropriate documents" (in this case "tax-sensitive" wills).**

Answer: Only the securities ($275,000) would have been governed by Tony's will ("W" in COW) and go into the bypass trust. The brokerage account, which is owned jointly, would have passed by operation of law ("O" in COW) to Carmela outright. Carmela would have also received Tony's bank account outright, as it passes by beneficiary designation (i.e. by contract, the "C" in COW) to Carmela. The end result would have been that the bypass trust would own the securities ($275,000) and Carmela would then own the house, bank accounts, and brokerage account, all of which total $1,075,000. Upon Carmela's subsequent demise, her estate would exceed the New Jersey estate tax threshold ($675,000), and, accordingly, her estate would be liable for New Jersey estate taxes totaling $37,400. Why weren't Tony and Carmela able to shelter $1,350,000 ($675,000 x two people) from New Jersey estate tax? They executed "tax-sensitive" wills. What went wrong? You got it—they did not retitle their assets ("asset titling").

In order to shelter $1,350,000 from New Jersey estate taxes, Tony and Carmela should have retitled their assets as follows:

OWNERSHIP OF ASSET

ASSET	JOINT	TONY	CARMELA
Brokerage Account (Stocks and Bonds)*		$200,00	$200,000
Bank Accounts**		$200,000	$75,000
Securities (Individually Owned)		$275,000	
House			$400,000

* Tony and Carmela closed their joint account and opened two individual accounts with no beneficiary designation.

** Tony and Carmela removed the "payable on death" designation from the bank accounts.

Now, upon Tony's demise, Tony's brokerage account, bank account, and securities (totaling $675,000) would have all passed by his will into the bypass trust benefiting Carmela. Remember, Carmela would have total access to the assets in the bypass trust, but when she subsequently dies, those assets would not be part of her estate.

Once again, although the federal and state estate tax Exemptions are increasing or will be eliminated, the importance of asset titling and executing the appropriate documents remains.

So, I ask you again, have you done your estate planning?

1. Do you have a **health-care directive**? Does it contain HIPPA, and did you appoint a successor medical agent?

2. Do you have a **power of attorney**? Does it contain a gifting provision, and did you appoint a successor financial agent?

3. Do you have a **will**?

4. Have you done your **asset titling**?

If you answered no to any of the foregoing questions, then you have not done your estate planning. However, now that you understand (1) what estate planning means and (2) how to effectuate it, you are armed with the knowledge to properly get it done.

CHAPTER 6

WHY IT'S NEVER TOO LATE TO TAKE ACTION

A s with most people, my family's experience when I was a kid had an enormous influence on my life. It helped me realize that I want to spend my days making sure other families don't go through what mine did. But as challenging as my parents' experience was, we made it through. My parents were able to put together a plan that allowed us to financially survive, even though the accident had left my father with no future earnings ability.

The insurance company paid him a small lump sum of money, and this was the foundation for my parent's new financial plan. They didn't put it back into the market where it could be dwindled away because of market losses or bad timing. Instead, they built a low-risk strategy for preservation. They used the insurance money to create a backup for my mother's income. They managed to keep their heads above water.

BETTER LATE THAN NEVER

The key is to get started as soon as you can. The Aegon 2013 Retirement Readiness Survey found that while 66 percent of respondents know they need to have a plan for retirement, only 12 percent have one they feel is good enough to take them safely through retirement. Twenty-four percent of women have no plan at all.[25] The Employee Benefit Research Institute found even more bad news: only 22 percent of workers are very confident they will have enough money in retirement, while 64 percent say they know they are behind where they should be with their savings. About 57 percent have saved less than $25,000, and almost a third have less than $1,000.[26]

If you're worried you haven't done all that you should to get ready for your retirement—or even if you *know* you haven't—don't be like a deer frozen in the headlights as your retirement gets nearer and nearer with each passing day. Take action *now*! There are still things you can do to get yourself back on course. Here are some better-late-than-never strategies for retirement planning.

CONSULT WITH A TRUSTED ADVISOR.

In other words, get help. You don't have to do this by yourself—and it will be a lot easier if you have an expert who can guide you. If you came in my office and took my financial stress test, and we discovered you had some major gaps in your retirement plan, we'd sit down and work out a plan to get you back on track. Even if you'd made some

25 Aegon 2013 Retirement Survey, Aegon, http://www.aegon.com/en/Home/Research/Aegon-Retirement-Readiness-Survey-20131/.

26 Gail Marks Jarvis, "Americans Ill-Prepared for Retirement, Survey Finds," *Chicago Tribune*, April 22, 2015, http://www.chicagotribune.com/business/yourmoney/ct-marksjarvis-0422-biz-20150421-column.html.

irreversible investments, there are always strategies for maximizing what you have to work with for your retirement income.

RUN THE NUMBERS AND GET THE FACTS.

You may not want to even think about your retirement, because you know you're not prepared and it scares you. But scary or not, the first thing you need to do is take a look at what your retirement needs are going to be. Make a list of all your expenses, as we've discussed earlier in this book. Once you have a good idea of what you're actually going to need, you'll be able to match that with a plan—and then take action.

REDUCE YOUR LIFESTYLE NOW SO THAT YOU CAN SAVE MORE.

A lot of Americans have gotten in the habit of spending more than they earn, which means that the dollars that could have been used to fund their retirements are paying off their credit cards instead. Stop spending your retirement money, and start saving it. Don't see this as a negative thing, something that puts unpleasant restrictions on your life. Ask yourself, "What do I really want my retirement to look like? How do I want to live? What is my time frame for achieving that?" If you set yourself goals for the future, you'll be more motivated to do the things you need to do today to achieve those goals.

Even small changes in your spending habits can make a big difference to your savings. Say you are fifty years old, and you know you haven't put away enough for your retirement. If you retire when you're seventy, and if you could cut just $10 out of your spending habits each and every day of those twenty years—for example, by bringing your lunch to work or eating at home at night instead of going out—those dollars could grow to $227,000 in twenty years if they were in an investment vehicle that earned a 10 percent annual return. If you were to save as much as $15 a day, the results could be as high as $342,000. Of course, what we're really talking about here is saving an extra $300 to $450 a month—but you may find it a lot easier to do if you set the money aside daily rather than monthly.

FATTEN UP YOUR 401(K) RETIREMENT ACCOUNT OR IRA.

For this strategy, I suggest you look at your workday and decide that for one hour out of each day you'll think of yourself as working for your retirement life instead of your current life. Say you make $50,000 a year, which means you make about $25 an hour. Every workday you'd give one hour to your retirement, which would mean you'd contribute $25 to your retirement account. This would add up to $125 a week or $6,500 a year.

INCREASE YOUR INCOME NOW SO YOU HAVE MORE TO SAVE FOR RETIREMENT.

Think about what you can do to make more money. Can you work more hours? Get a part-time job? Maybe even put off retirement for a year to ensure you have what you need for the rest of your life?

TAKE ADVANTAGE OF YOUR EMPLOYER'S RETIREMENT SAVINGS MATCH.

If your employer will match your contribution to a 401(k) up to a certain percentage of your salary, make sure you're contributing at least that much. Say you earn $50,000 a year and your employer will match your contributions to a 401(k) up to 3 percent of your income. That means that if you contribute at least $1,500 to your 401(k), your employer will kick in another $1,500. If you work another twenty years, your employer's contribution could mount up to another $30,000 toward your retirement fund.

IF YOU'RE OVER FIFTY, TAKE ADVANTAGE OF IRA AND 401(K) CATCH-UP OPTIONS.

The law allows older workers a higher ceiling for maximum contributions. Put in as much as you legally can each year.

PAY OFF DEBTS.

After you've set up an ongoing plan that contributes the maximum amount possible to your retirement fund, make paying off any high-interest credit card debt your next priority. You don't want to still be carrying the weight of this debt around your neck during retirement.

PUT YOUR RETIREMENT FIRST, AHEAD OF YOUR KIDS' COLLEGE EDUCATION.

Ideally, of course, you probably want to do both. But if you can only afford to do one, choose your retirement. This isn't as selfish as it might sound. The chances of you one day being a financial burden on your adult children will be greatly reduced if you have adequately prepared for your retirement years. Besides, there are good loans offered for college education—but not for retirement.

START A SIDE BUSINESS.

Do you have a hobby you could turn into a business? If you love to cook, could you do catering on the weekends? If you're an expert in your field, could you start doing consulting work? If you love to salvage antiques, could you set up a shop where you offer your services to others? If you love to do crafts, could you sell them at craft fairs and on Etsy? Is there an online business that interests you? A part-time business can increase your income now, giving you the ability to save more for retirement. It might make you qualified to open additional retirement savings accounts with higher savings thresholds, allowing you to save more. It could also give you an additional ongoing income stream after you've retired from your full-time job.

BE STRATEGIC ABOUT SOCIAL SECURITY.

Waiting to collect Social Security until you're older could be a good strategy for increasing your retirement income.

Full retirement age—when you're eligible to receive full Social Security benefits—was once sixty-five for everyone, but over the years, that's changed. Social Security law continues to change, so make sure you work with your financial advisor to determine what's best for you under the current law.

TAKE OUT A DISABILITY INSURANCE POLICY.

If you were to become physically unable to perform the duties of your job, disability insurance would pay you a percentage of your monthly income. This is a good way to protect the funds you have already saved from the risk of a crisis—like the one my family faced—that might otherwise mean you'd need to dip deep into your retirement savings.

DOWNSIZE YOUR LIVING EXPENSES.

If you are still paying a mortgage, selling your home and moving into a much smaller place could decrease your spending significantly— and add to your ability to save for retirement. Even if you own your home, you still might be able to save money on utilities by moving to a smaller place, while at the same time using the money you make on the sale of your home as a contribution to your retirement funds. Keep in mind the big picture, though, and do your math. How much will daily life (including such factors as transportation costs, groceries, and utilities) cost in your new home? If you're moving into a smaller house that is in an area where the cost of living is significantly higher than where you live now, you might find you're not saving as much as you had thought you would. On the other hand, moving where the cost of living is lower (for example, moving out of a city and into the country) could enhance your downsizing efforts.

PROTECT WHATEVER RETIREMENT SAVINGS YOU HAVE AGAINST PRINCIPAL LOSS.

To put this another way: don't gamble with your retirement money! If you have put most of your retirement savings into the stock market or a savings vehicle that's based on the stock market (such as mutual funds), you could see sizable losses when the market goes down.

Over long periods of time, the stock markets have outperformed real estate, bonds, gold, and almost all other asset classes, but despite its good long-term track record, the stock market is volatile. Let's say over the thirty years of your working career you saved $500,000 for retirement. Now you're sixty-four, and you're planning to retire in one more year—when suddenly the bottom falls out of the stock market (as historically happens from time to time). If you lost 37 percent in one year, you would lose $185,000. You don't have time left to make that money back.

Today's market volatility makes it difficult to predict what will be happening when it comes time for you to retire—and if you're close to retirement age, you may not have time to wait out the market. I've worked with retirees who lost money in variable annuities, mutual funds, stocks, bonds, commodities, and commodity funds. I've also worked with retirees who, in their quest to generate retirement income, bought investment real estate. Unfortunately, due to plunging real estate prices in many markets, a number of these retirees lost a significant portion of their retirement assets. All these retirees were seeking to secure an even higher income during retirement—but they gambled and lost. They invested their money in something other than a vehicle that can generate guaranteed lifetime income, and they opted instead for higher "maybe income."

The irony of this is that in a number of cases I've seen throughout the years, those retirees who went for "maybe income" ended up receiving little or no income from these risky or nonguaranteed investments. Instead, they ended up living off whatever money they had left after their investment losses. They'd *hoped* their investments would go up in value. If their investments didn't go up in value, as so many stocks and so much real estate don't, they'd *hoped* they would at least stay about flat. And if their investments started to decline in value, they'd *hoped* they would not lose too much in value. Unfortunately, "hope" is not a valid investment strategy. So if you find yourselves doing a lot of hoping about your retirement investments, that could be a warning sign that you're taking too many risks with your money. You might want to seriously reconsider how much of your retirement funds you expose to that risk. If you depend on your retirement assets to pay your bills or support your lifestyle, make sure your money is protected.

MAKE SURE YOUR RETIREMENT SAVINGS ARE SOMEWHERE THEY ARE GROWING ENOUGH TO GET YOU THE INCOME YOU'LL NEED.

I know I just said not to gamble with your retirement money. But you also want to make sure your money can grow. With interest on savings accounts so low, you might as well bury your money in your backyard or stick it under your mattress. Very few retirees have so much money that they can sit on it. They need it to grow in order to have the income they'll need throughout their retirement. A good financial advisor will be able to talk to you about guaranteed-income investments in annuities.

GET STARTED NOW!

This strategy is the most important of all. If you're behind on your retirement planning, the single most important thing you can do is get started immediately. Don't put it off any longer. The sooner you start, the greater your possible retirement income will be. This is the time to get it right. You owe it to yourself.

CONCLUSION

I t's time for you to sit down and get honest with yourself. Are you absolutely certain you have the retirement plan you need? How healthy is your financial outlook? Do you have a holistic plan that takes all factors into consideration?

Remember what I said earlier: a plan isn't diversification. It's not enough to have domestic and international mutual funds and stocks. And it's not enough to have a growth fund and an income fund. That alone doesn't make a plan.

We're in some very unprecedented times economically. International wars, domestic issues, environmental issues, politics . . . the list of factors that affect our economy could go on and on. Meanwhile, pensions are going broke, and more and more people are going to have to build their own private pension funds.

Perhaps more than ever before, it's vital that you sit down with a trusted advisor and make sure your retirement plan is in good shape. When you build a house, what do you start with? The foundation.

Your foundation should be investment strategies with minimal risk that will give you a guaranteed income throughout your retirement years, no matter how long you live. Once you have that in place, then you can build the rest of your house, knowing that the foundation is solid. Stocks and mutual funds and other forms of riskier investments could be the walls and the roof of your house. Granted, if a hurricane comes along, it could cause some serious damage to your house—but so long as you have a good foundation where you can take shelter, you'll be safe. You'll be able to weather even the worst storms. In financial terms, even if you lose some investments to the stock market, make sure you still have a guaranteed income, drawn from safer investment vehicles, that will continue to cover your basic needs. It's okay if it turns out you can't take the cruise to the Bahamas, so long as you *can* pay for your groceries and utilities and all your other basic needs.

In a sense, you need to think of it as a "personal pension." What is a personal pension as opposed to, say, having bank savings accounts set aside or a portfolio of investment accounts? Well, savings and portfolios are assets whose strengths lie at opposite ends of the financial spectrum, from protected principal to growth potential. However, for income purposes, neither one can provide assurance that your cost of living will be covered every year into the future or that your principal won't be eroded if you take withdrawals from an asset that goes up and down. A "personal pension" could offer you what an actual employer pension might provide—permanent "income" for life. Without setting up a strategy to accomplish this goal, you could find yourself short on the money you need to pay for basic needs in your later years.

WRITE IT DOWN

Don't make the mistake of thinking that a retirement plan is something you can keep in your head. Write it down!

Research has proven that when we put an action plan into writing, we're much more likely to achieve it.[27] Preparing for retirement is no different from anything else you hope to achieve. It takes knowing what your goals are—and then writing down a plan to make them happen.

As you get started on your plan, answer these questions. Some of them you can answer yourself, while others you should refer to when you sit down with an advisor.

- Do I have a trusted advisor?

- Do I need to get a second opinion?

- Is my financial advisor the right guide for my retirement?

- Do I understand today's economy?

- Am I truly engaged with my financial well-being?

- Do I understand how my life expectancy will impact my retirement?

- Do I know how much money I will need to retire?

- Do I have the documents I need for estate planning?

- Have I titled my assets appropriately?

- Am I certain my will is tax efficient?

- Have I set up my investments to be as tax efficient as possible?

- Do I understand how inflation will affect my retirement funds?

- Is my retirement strategy sufficiently diversified?

27 Gail Matthews, "Goals Research Summary," http://www.dominican.edu/academics/ahss/under-graduate-programs/psych/faculty/assets-gail-matthews/researchsummary2.pdf.

- Am I using the investment vehicles that are best suited to achieve my financial goals?

FINANCIAL HEALTH

Never forget that your financial health is essential to your well-being. Like your physical health, it will shape your future happiness, activity level, and lifestyle. And like your physical health, it also requires a holistic, broad perspective. There are no quick fixes, because each piece of your financial well-being contributes to and supports all the others. It will take time and effort to achieve a healthy retirement plan—but it is well worth your effort!

SELF-EVALUATION

Put a checkmark beside each statement that applies to you:

☐ I want to start planning my income for retirement. I don't like the way that sounds. I want to start planning my income for retirement, but I'm not even sure how much money I need to have before I can retire.

☐ I need help evaluating my portfolio and my expenses and figuring out what the best route to take in retirement might be.

☐ I think I may need to continue working at least part time to be able to afford my basic living expenses.

☐ I want to know how to maximize my Social Security income and when is the best time for me to start taking payments.

☐ I want a minimum monthly income and want to be sure it's there for me no matter what happens in the markets, and I'm not willing to sacrifice the security or principal that I have.

☐ I want to retain some control of my money so that I can use it without penalty if my situation changes. I want a plan that has an exit strategy.

☐ I want guidance as to which of my assets I should use first and how to optimize the funds I will use later.

☐ I want increasing income for retirement.

☐ I'm having trouble finding an advisor who is focused on my retirement goals.

☐ I want extra protection on my assets in case of illness.

☐ I'm concerned that I may need extra income for future health-care costs, and I want to look at the most cost-efficient options.

☐ I want tax-effective benefits.

☐ What if I die first? I want to make sure my family's stuff and heirs are financially protected, but I don't know how to guarantee that will happen or that it will happen in the most efficient manner.

If you checked off any of the questions on the worksheet, I can help you. Don't hesitate to give me a call!

—*Keith Gebert*

OUR SERVICES

IF YOU NEED ASSISTANCE DEVELOPING A FINANCIAL STRATEGY FOR YOUR FUTURE, RIGHTBRIDGE FINANCIAL GROUP OFFERS THE FOLLOWING SERVICES:

- RETIREMENT INCOME STRATEGIES
- WEALTH ACCUMULATION
- ASSET PROTECTION
- ANNUITIES
- LIFE INSURANCE
- TAX-MINIMIZATION STRATEGIES
- LONG-TERM CARE
- IRA AND 401(K) ROLLOVERS

TO TAKE YOUR OWN FREE "PORTFOLIO STRESS TEST," VISIT US ONLINE AT WWW.RIGHTBRIDGEFINANCIAL.COM.

PHONE: 855-500-RBFG (7234)

EMAIL: INFO@RIGHTBRIDGEFINANCIAL.COM

CPSIA information can be obtained
at www.ICGtesting.com
Printed in the USA
BVOW06*0904270117

474658BV00010B/362/P